PRAISE FOR
THE GHOST NEXT DOOR

"The Ghost Next Door *is a chilling collection of real ghost stories that will have readers sleeping with the lights on! I couldn't put it down!*"

—Leslie Rule, author of *Coast to Coast Ghosts*

"*Very well-written...a really good book...I thoroughly enjoyed it.*"

—Kriss Stephens of MTV's *FEAR*

"*An excellent example of how a collection of ghost stories should read...definitely not your run-of-the-mill (ghost) book...down-right creepy...DO NOT read this book alone in the dark—trust me!*"

—Vincent Wilson, host of *Paranormal Weekly*

"*Sure to shock and surprise you...highly recommended.*"

—AuthorZone.com

"*Entertaining and well-written...the author skillfully presents a wonderful book that you won't soon forget!*"

—Troy Taylor, author of *Spirits of the Civil War*
and president of the American Ghost Society

The Ghost Next Door

The Ghost Next Door

*True Stories of Paranormal Encounters
from Everyday People*

Mark Alan Morris

iUniverse Star
New York Lincoln Shanghai

The Ghost Next Door
True Stories of Paranormal Encounters from Everyday People

iUniverse Star
an iUniverse, Inc. imprint

For information address:
iUniverse, Inc.
2021 Pine Lake Road, Suite 100
Lincoln, NE 68512
www.iuniverse.com

ISBN: 0-595-29786-2

Printed in the United States of America

For Ann, with whom I read my first ghost stories

Contents

Acknowledgements

I would like to extend my sincerest thanks to all who contributed their stories to this collection; it would not, of course, have been possible without them. Credit goes also to Diane Bryan, who acted as a liaison between myself and some of my sources; her persistence is much appreciated. I would like to thank my wonderful wife, who patiently tolerated the many hours I spent in our study, huddled over the computer. And lastly, I would like to express my gratitude to Mrs. Docia Schultz Williams, whose book entitled *Spirits of San Antonio and South Texas* placed the proverbial "bug in my ear" to undertake this project years before I actually started it.

Introduction

Like millions of other Americans, I have always been fascinated by ghosts. I can remember shuddering with anticipatory delight as a young boy at the mere mention of the word, knowing there might soon be a spooky tale unfolding for my intrigued little ears to absorb. Over the years, my interest in the subject of ghosts and the paranormal has remained constant, perhaps even growing a bit deeper as maturity allows me progressive insight into the more intellectual aspects of this phenomenon.

I must confess that I personally have never actually *seen* a ghost (as far as I know), nor have I ever really had an experience of my own that could be construed as "paranormal". But several of my friends—and even a few of my family members—claim that *they* have. My lack of personal experience with ghosts, however, does nothing to dissuade me from entertaining the thought that they may exist. I, for one, am not so arrogant as to believe there is nothing left in this world that cannot be explained or understood, even in *this* day and age. Our definition of "the unknown" is, after all, subjective; it has changed over the centuries as one mystery after another has been solved through the advent and evolution of scientific investigation.

Obviously, the realm of the unknown has diminished considerably in the time since mankind's humble beginnings, but it certainly hasn't vanished altogether; we are still far from having it "all figured out". We are afforded the luxury of looking back at some of the "great enigmas" of the past with amusement, because we now know the explanation behind them. But, conversely, imagine for a moment what would happen if someone who lived a few hundred years ago were to somehow catch a glimpse of *our* world—a modern-day passenger jet flying overhead, for instance. While to us an airliner is just another mode of transportation, our friend from the past would no doubt be unable to comprehend or explain it, and would therefore be resigned to dismissing it as either the product of an overactive imagination or simply a great, unsolvable mystery. I think it's safe to assume that he would probably also be *afraid* of it. In short, we tend to fear the most that which we understand the least.

Perhaps one day we will be able to fully comprehend and explain the phenomenon of ghosts, perhaps not. For now, it seems there are as many varying beliefs and theories about these spectral entities as there are witnesses to them. The most popular belief seems to be that ghosts are the disembodied spirits of the dead, still somehow bound to the realm of the living. Another explanation is that ghostly apparitions are merely past events that were somehow "recorded" into the environment and are "replayed" from time to time for whatever reason. One of the more recent theories is that ghosts are projections of our own consciousness—visible thoughts, if you will. Of course, it's possible that there are multiple types of hauntings and therefore more than one accurate explanation, but my inclination is to side with the majority on this particular matter.

To elaborate a bit on my own personal speculation about ghosts, it seems to me that, rather than being solely a matter of chance or coincidence, the probability of a person encountering a ghost during his or her lifetime depends largely upon that person's *sensitivity* to ghosts. It's a simple and logical answer to the common question, "Why do some people see ghosts while others don't?" It seems likely to me that there would be varying degrees of sensitivity to this phenomenon just as there are to light, sound, touch, smell and taste.

I suppose what I'm referring to here is the proverbial *sixth sense*—the faculty which detects otherworldly elements; a kind of "revenant radar". Just as is true of the other five senses, the sixth appears to vary in strength from person to person. Judging from my own track record of *zero* ghostly encounters, my sixth sense seems to be decidedly underdeveloped; on the flipside, a certain friend of mine has had enough run-ins with spirits to strongly suggest that *hers* is considerably well-evolved. This brings up the question of whether there is any way for those of us who are "paranormally challenged" to develop our sixth sense; well…that will have to be another book.

Explanations aside, there is certainly no shortage of people who share my interest in this topic and who no doubt derive a certain amount of pleasure from curling up in their favorite armchair with a volume of ghost stories, preferably on a stormy night. Having done so myself on many occasions and having also made the acquaintance of several people over the years who've had first-hand experiences with the supernatural, it occurred to me that putting together my *own* collection of ghostly tales might be both a plausible and interesting project. I was right.

At first, I was concerned that I might have some degree of difficulty in obtaining enough material to comprise an entire book. My doubt quickly subsided, however, when I began querying friends and acquaintances on the matter and subsequently realized just how *common* ghostly encounters seem to be. In fact, based on my research, it appears that *most people* have had some kind of unexplainable experience at some point in their lives, or know someone who has. This somewhat unsettling discovery led me to realize that the spirit world may be a lot closer to home than I had imagined—hence, the title of this book.

As I collected these stories through in-person, telephone and e-mail interviews, I became aware of certain aspects that were repeated through several of them—you'll no doubt notice this yourself as you progress through the book. Not only do these shared characteristics serve to mutually substantiate the stories, they also seem to enhance the mystery surrounding ghosts in general. For example, many spectral visitations seem to occur around 3:00 a.m.; loud, knocking sounds are often heard; "cold spots" are felt in certain areas; household items inexplicably disappear, only to reappear some time later. If you've been privy to a fair amount of ghost stories, these things may sound familiar to you; they are common threads that run through many accounts of paranormal activity, from the most famous cases to the obscure instances revealed here for the first time.

The following stories were recounted to me by normal, everyday people from all walks of life—family members, friends, coworkers and acquaintances—who have, at one time or another, experienced something they consider to be paranormal. I do not attempt to validate, confirm or vouch for any of the information presented here; I merely offer it for your consideration and entertainment. I will, however, state that there is no reason why any of the contributors would have given me falsified or fabricated information; they would have gained nothing from doing so. No incentives were offered or given, monetary or otherwise. In fact, a few of my "sources" were somewhat uneasy at first about "going public" with their experiences for fear that it might somehow reflect unfavorably upon them (some names have been changed by request). No, these individuals generously agreed to share their stories simply as a favor to me.

So make sure all your doors are locked, grab a snack, settle into your favorite chair and enjoy. Oh—and if you happen to hear a strange noise while you're reading, don't worry…it's probably just a passing airliner…

The Haunted Hotel

Ghosts and hauntings have traditionally been associated with older structures or locations. This seems only logical; the older a structure is, the more history it has; the more history, the greater the chance of there having been an occurrence at some point from which a haunting may have originated. The following story involves just such a structure, with more than its share of history...and ghosts.

A few years ago, my friend and colleague Karen Gentry-Sizemore had a strange experience while she and a coworker were attending a work-related seminar in San Antonio, Texas. Accommodations had been arranged for them at the famed Menger Hotel, which is located very near The Alamo.

Founded in 1859, the Menger is renowned for its colorful history, its elegance and its impressive list of famous patrons. Among the more notable guests are short story writer O. Henry (who was fond of the hotel and included it in several of his works), General Robert E. Lee (who—legend has it—once rode his horse into the hotel lobby), General Ulysses S. Grant, President Dwight D. Eisenhower, Lilly Langtry and Mae West.

Unbeknownst to Karen at the time of her arrival, the Menger Hotel is also reputed to be the permanent residence of several ghosts.

◆   ◆   ◆

During a recent interview, Karen revealed that, although she knew nothing of the hotel's history or reputation, she could feel a "very strange presence" immediately upon entering the building.

"We put our suitcases in our rooms and left to go to a meeting," Karen recalled. "When we came back, I found that my suitcase had been opened up and my things were spread out as if someone had gone through them. I thought it might have been a member of the house-keeping staff, so I went down to the front desk and asked if anyone had been in my room. They assured me that no one had. I told them about my suitcase, but they had no explanation for it."

When Karen told me this, it really didn't surprise me. It seemed to me that, if the culprit *had* been someone from housekeeping, he or she surely would have been careful to replace everything exactly as it was found so as not to arouse suspicion. But the suitcase was found opened and Karen's things were scattered…almost as if the guilty party *wanted* her to know that someone had been there.

"I went back up to my room, put my things back in order, and got ready for bed," she continued. "After I brushed my teeth, I left the bathroom door open and the light on so I'd have some light in the room. As soon as I got into bed, *the light went out and the door closed*. I got up to see if there was an air vent or something that might have blown the door shut—although I didn't know how that could have affected the light. I opened the door, looked around and found that there was no air vent blowing and no other reason why the door would've closed on its own. There was certainly no reason for the *light* to have gone out. At first, I thought the bulb might have burned out, but I found that the light switch was in the 'off' position and, when I flipped it up, the light came back on.

"So again, I left the light on and the door open and got back into bed. A few seconds later, *it happened again*. The light went out. The door closed.

"I got up and repeated the same inspection routine—more thor-oughly this time—then climbed back into bed. Seconds later, it was the same scene. For the *third* time in a row, the light went out and the door closed by itself.

"At that point, the *closet* door began to *open*. I just said, 'Okay, you win—just leave me alone...I just want to sleep!'"

Karen mused that her statement must have satisfied whatever was in the room with her, because nothing else happened that night. I remarked to her that most people in that situation probably would have hurriedly packed up their things and asked for a different room, or left the hotel entirely.

"If anything else had happened that night, I probably would have," she admitted.

◆   ◆   ◆

Although the remainder of that night passed uneventfully, something happened the following morning that *did* prompt Karen to leave the hotel—two days early, in fact, causing her to miss two of the three days of the seminar.

"I had gone into a small restroom on the second floor, above the lobby," she explained. "There were only two stalls, and they were both open when I went in, so it was obvious that I was alone in there. But, when I came out of my stall, I was startled to see a woman standing beside the sink, staring at me. I wasn't expecting to see anyone since I hadn't heard anyone else come in. The woman was probably in her late twenties or early thirties, with brownish hair and fair skin, and she was wearing what looked like an old-fashioned maid's uniform.

"She was staring at me intensely with this strange expression on her face and—never breaking eye contact—she asked, 'Did you sleep well last night?' I was very uncomfortable, but I managed to say 'yes'—which, of course, was a lie. She continued with, 'So...you're enjoying your stay here?' I lied again and said I was. Then—and this was *really* creepy—she asked, '*Are you sure?*'

"That was enough for me...I excused myself and got out of there in a hurry. It was so weird—just the way she was looking at me and the things she was saying gave me the creeps. It was like she was hinting that she knew what had happened to me the previous night. Of course, there's no way she could have known...*unless she had been there.*"

Karen admitted that, in retrospect, she believes the woman in the restroom may indeed have been a visible manifestation of the spirit that was in her room the previous evening. Shortly after the restroom incident, Karen located her traveling companion and convinced him that they should check out of the hotel that day.

"Since there were no other hotels with vacancies in town," she explained, "we left San Antonio and headed back to Dallas."

> *What unseen force was responsible for the strange activity in Karen's hotel room that night? Who was the mysterious woman in the restroom? Were they one and the same? Karen doubts she'll ever find out...she doesn't plan to return to the Menger Hotel...*

NOTE: A few weeks after writing this story, I was perusing an Internet site that listed haunted locations throughout the country, along with a brief description of each. While examining the "Texas" listings, I noticed the Menger Hotel was included. Curious, I read the paragraph beneath the heading. The first among the ghosts mentioned was that of a maid who was murdered there long ago and now wanders the upper floors...

Strange Doings at the Parker House

Boston, Massachusetts is one of our country's oldest cities; consequently, it boasts a rich and colorful history. As we discovered in the previous story, along with history usually come at least a few resident spirits. Ask anyone who has stayed a night or two in the Parker House Hotel, and you'll likely get confirmation...

Located near Boston's theater district stands the Parker House, the nation's oldest continually operating hotel. Founded in 1855 by Harvey D. Parker, the elegant hotel in its heyday provided fine dining and accommodations for some of the most prominent figures of America's Golden Age of Literature. Writers such as Emerson, Thoreau, Hawthorne and Longfellow met regularly for conversation and camaraderie in the legendary 19th-century Saturday Club.

Over the next century-and-a-half, the hotel has been visited (and frequented) by former presidents Ulysses S. Grant, Franklin D. Roosevelt, John F. Kennedy and Bill Clinton. A number of celebrated sports figures, stars of stage and screen, and other celebrities—infamous as well as famous—have also been guests.

◆　　◆　　◆

My attention was first drawn to the Parker House Hotel when my coworker Pete Bryant told me of an unusual experience he once had there.

"As you know, I used to be a flight attendant," Pete began. "Several years ago, I was overnighting at the Parker House. At one point that evening, I decided to take a walk down the hall and get a soda from the drink machine there. Well, as I was putting my first quarter in the slot, the machine suddenly went black—the moment I touched it. When I pulled the coin away, the machine came back to life. The next time I attempted to put the quarter in, everything functioned normally.

"So I made my selection and leaned over to pick up the can. Out of the corner of my eye, I saw what appeared to be a female figure dressed in a flowing gown walking—or rather 'floating'—quickly past the door that led into the vending area. I didn't think much of it at the time; I figured I would find this person waiting for the elevator in the foyer since I hadn't heard the elevator chime. But, as I walked past the waiting area, I was surprised to find that *it was empty*. There was no sign of the woman…or anyone else, for that matter. I also caught the scent of perfume as I was walking back to my room. I later learned from the front desk personnel that the 3rd floor—the floor I was staying on—is notorious for strange happenings."

◆   ◆   ◆

My curiosity piqued, I contacted the Parker House staff for more information. A few days later, I received a telephone call from the Guest Service Manager of the hotel—we'll call him "Shawn"—who has worked there for the past 25 years. During our conversation, he divulged information on the hotel's history and described some of the strange occurrences that have taken place—and still take place—within its walls.

"The original building was constructed in 1855," Shawn explained. "In 1886, a new section was added; because it faced Bosworth Street, this portion later became known as the 'Bosworth section'. The final and most recent addition to the hotel was built in 1927.

"Late one night, several years ago, one of our security guards was making his rounds in the Bosworth section. He was walking along a deserted hallway when he happened to glance to his right and saw on the wall what appeared to be the shadow of a gentleman wearing a top hat. Well, he really didn't think anything about it, just that there must've been someone walking behind him, casting the shadow. So he stepped aside to let the man pass, only to discover that there was no one there. He was so upset by the incident that he refused to go back to that part of the hotel. In fact, we finally had to terminate his employment with us—we needed a security guard who would patrol *all* areas of the hotel, of course.

"There's also something strange about the third floor. There's one particular elevator in the building that's always being mysteriously called to that floor. It stops there quite a bit. As you're going up in the elevator, it'll stop at the third floor and, when the doors open, there's just nobody there. This has happened countless times over the years and has been investigated on several occasions, but there is never any explanation—mechanical or otherwise.

"There are two theories about the elevator; one is that it's haunted by the ghost of Charles Dickens, who stayed on the third floor in 1867 and 1868; the other is that it's the spirit of Charlotte Cushman, who lived in the Dickens suite in the 1870s."

Shawn continued with a story about a particular room that seemed to be another source of paranormal activity.

"I believe it was room 1007. That's one of our 'airline rooms'. We have certain rooms we set aside for airline employees—flight attendants and pilots. Anyway, we sometimes get complaints from the men and women who stay in that room overnight. Usually, they're reports of strange sounds coming from somewhere in the room—sounds of someone rocking back and forth in a rocking chair all night. The weird thing is that there isn't even a rocking chair in that room."

◆   ◆   ◆

My continued investigation into the history of the Parker House revealed more accounts of mysterious happenings. For instance, there are those who believe the ghost of Harvey Parker himself roams the halls on the tenth floor annex. Many sightings have been reported, one of which happened around 1950. A woman reported seeing an apparition outside room 1078. She described it as first appearing as 'a kind of mist' in the air, which slowly took on the form of a heavy-set older man with a black mustache. The figure turned in her direction and stared directly at her for a moment, then vanished. Shaken, the woman hurriedly made her way down to the front desk and reported what she had seen to the staff. Security guards were dispatched to the tenth floor but, after a thorough search, could find nothing.

Then there's the man who died in room 303 back in 1949. Stories of bewildered tenants who encounter the inexplicable scent of whiskey while staying in that room continue to circulate at the hotel.

Chances are there have been countless other occurrences in the many years since the Parker House first opened its doors that have gone unreported. It's probable that many unlucky guests who've had ghostly encounters during their stay at the hotel have elected not to tell anyone, leaving us only to speculate about the true extent of the paranormal activity there. No one man, it seems, will ever know *all* the secrets of the Parker House Hotel—except maybe for Mr. Parker…

Apparitions that wander the hallways…elevators that stop by themselves…inexplicable sounds and smells…these are all part of the history and mystery of the Parker House Hotel. Perhaps Oliver Wendell Holmes said it best in the words of his poem "At The Saturday Club":

Such guests! What famous names
its record boasts, whose owners wander
in the mob of ghosts!

The Ghostly Bride

Hauntings are often the result of tragic events; the residual bitterness of a wrongdoing can be carried to the grave, sometimes leading to a restless earthbound spirit. In the dead of night, these long-forgotten tragedies are suddenly and horrifically revealed to unwary and unwilling spectators who just happen to be in the right place at the wrong time...

During my telephone interview with Shawn, the Guest Service Manager for the Parker House Hotel, he hinted that he might have a ghost story of his own. After a bit of prodding, he shared with me an uncanny tale, which took place years ago and miles away from the Parker House.

"I grew up in a very old house," Shawn told me. "As a result of pecking order, I got the single room up in the attic by myself. We didn't have air conditioning in the house, so it would sometimes get quite uncomfortable up there during the warm season.

"One summer night when I was about sixteen or seventeen, it was so hot up in my room I just couldn't stand it. So, around one o'clock in the morning, I decided to go downstairs. I went into the living room and collapsed on the loveseat. I didn't bother to turn on any lights.

"I hadn't been there long when I sensed that someone was sitting beside me. I looked to my left and saw the image of a woman in a wedding dress sitting there. No sooner had I seen the woman than, out of the corner of my eye, I saw the figure of a man dressed as a minister standing in front of the loveseat. He was wearing one of those old-fashioned brown hats and everything. He was muttering something like, 'You could marry my daughter.' I just sat there, frozen. Then he began reciting, *'Dearly beloved, we are gathered here today...'*

"All I could think was that I must've been dreaming, so I jumped up and ran to the kitchen sink to splash water on my face. But, just before I got to the sink, the man appeared in front of me again, repeating, *'Dearly beloved, we are gathered here today...'* I looked to my left and there *she* was again—the woman in the wedding dress—standing next to me. So I ran past the minister—or rather *through* him—and back up to my attic bedroom. I got under the covers—because ghosts can't get you when you're under the covers—and tried to forget about the heat. Eventually, I fell asleep.

"By the next morning, I wasn't sure whether it was real or if I had dreamt the whole thing. I decided not to tell anybody for fear that they might think I was crazy."

◆   ◆   ◆

Shawn went on to tell me that he eventually found out the cause of his experience that summer night.

"Years later," he continued, "I was having a drink with my sister and we were talking about that house. At one point, she asked me if I knew the history of the house. I told her I didn't and asked her to fill me in. She told me that there was a young woman living there long ago *who was jilted on her wedding day.* For years afterwards, she never left the house.

"There was no electricity in the house back then, and folks would sometimes see her at night, walking through the house holding a candle. She died in the room that became my sister's room after my family moved in.

"My sister went on to tell me about something strange that had happened to *her* in the house. She said it happened one night after she broke up with her boyfriend. She was laying on her bed, crying, when she heard the distinct sound of a woman cackling right there in the room with her."

It seems as though you never know when or where you'll run into a ghost. After hearing Shawn's story, I couldn't help but wonder what would have happened if he had stuck around for the rest of the ceremony...

La Muerte

Some people say the ability to see ghosts is hereditary—a kind of legacy passed down through the generations. Presumably, there is some debate among these individuals as to whether this ability is a blessing or a curse. Perceptions aside, the following tale certainly seems to be a good argument for the theory…

After hearing from a mutual friend about my quest for ghost stories, my coworker Hal Prestridge came forward with an intriguing story of his ongoing experiences with the supernatural.

"My first experience learning about ghosts was when I was very young," Hal remembered. "When I was four or five years old, I spent the night with my great-grandmother. I was scared to death because she was 'old and scary'. She was from Mexico, and moved to San Antonio, Texas in the early 1900s. I remember that her bed was made in the old style, with a hand-sewn mattress suspended from rope. She always used to sit in her rocking chair at night with all the lights out and smoke homemade cigarettes, rolled in corn shucks.

"It was very dark that night as she rocked back and forth in her chair; all I could see were the red embers glowing at the tip of her cigarette. After a while, she cleared her throat and said, *'Alguna vez has visto la muerte?'* which means, *'Do you ever see the dead?'* Well, I didn't even know what dead people were, so I said no. She then told me that if I *did* ever see the dead, I shouldn't be scared—they've just come to make sure I'm all right. She told me they usually appear at the end of the bed, and might speak to me. Needless to say, I didn't sleep at all that night and would frequently glance toward the foot of the bed."

It seemed to me that Hal's great-grandmother was preparing him for things to come. Judging from her apparent nonchalance regarding the subject of ghosts and her seeming familiarity with their habits, I got the distinct impression that she'd had at least a few visitations *herself* during her lifetime.

◆   ◆   ◆

"My first actual encounter with a ghost took place in 1968, while I was living with my parents and grandparents," Hal explained. "My bedroom had two single beds and I always slept in the one nearest the door. One night, I hadn't been asleep long when I woke up to find a woman leaning over my bed, staring down at me. When I looked at her face, I saw no features; it was more like I was looking up into the night sky. For some reason, I wasn't afraid and I sat up in my bed. As I did this, the woman stood up, went over to the other bed and sat down. She put her hands across her face as if she were crying.

"I got out of bed and started to walk toward the woman to find out what was making her so sad. As my feet touched the floor, she got up and walked out the door. It wasn't until after she was gone that I realized she hadn't walked, but rather *floated* out of the room. The woman's figure was very similar to my mother's, so my first assumption was that my mother had been in my room and was checking on me. I went into her bedroom and asked what she needed. She had obviously been fast asleep and told me to repeat myself. I asked her again if she'd been in my room. She assured me that she hadn't. This left me confused, but not afraid."

◆   ◆   ◆

Hal told me that nothing special happened over the next few months except that, by that time, his younger sister had moved into the room with him and occupied the other bed.

"Around that time," he recalled, "I started feeling cool breezes float across my face while lying in bed at night. I would open my eyes to find nothing there. One night, after a couple of nights of feeling this, I heard a faint voice call my name. I squinted into the darkness and saw the same woman who had been leaning over my bed before. This time, she was standing outside the doorway, peeking into the room. She stood there a few seconds, then faded away. This happened on more than one occasion and I'd always get up to check the hallway, but never found anyone there. I had no idea who this woman was.

"Several nights passed and she didn't reappear. Then one night, as I was lying in bed, I saw a gray shadow materialize just above my feet. It was the mysterious woman I'd been seeing—but she was only visible from the neck up. I decided to try and speak to the woman, but as I started to, the shadowy head shot toward the ceiling and then burst into something like fireworks."

◆   ◆   ◆

Hal went on to tell me that he eventually moved out of the house. One might logically assume that this would put an end to his supernatural encounters. I soon learned, however, that this was not the case.

"I was sharing a place with a friend," Hal continued. "My grandmother and my friend's grandfather had recently passed away in the same month. One evening, we had friends over and we were all sitting around the living room, enjoying some pleasant conversation. It was getting late when we somehow got on the subject of ghosts. Just as one of our friends started to ask about the ghost I had seen many years before, all the lights in the house started to flicker. They had never done that before…and they haven't since. When they quit flickering, a couple of sympathy cards I had put on an old standup Victrola rose into the air and floated to the center of the room. The cards hung there in the air for a few seconds, then fell to the ground.

"It couldn't have been a breeze or a draft because the cards rose *straight up* into the air, midway between the Victrola and the ceiling, then moved *horizontally* across the room. Needless to say, our visiting friends were scared to death, but we managed to calm them down and talk them out of leaving. Of course, we changed the topic of conversation and didn't talk about ghosts anymore that evening."

♦   ♦   ♦

It would seem that either the spirit Hal encountered before leaving home had somehow followed him to his new location, or he just happened to move into *another* haunted residence. Either way, this was not to be the last of his encounters.

"For years after the sympathy card incident," Hal recalled, "I didn't see or hear anything out of the ordinary. Then one day, recently, I had another experience. I had bought one of those 'computer cameras' that you mount on your computer monitor so that you and a friend with a similar setup can see each other as you're chatting online. One evening, after I'd been using it for several days, I was chatting online with a friend when our connection was suddenly lost.

"Now, when you lose your connection or intentionally disconnect, you see *yourself* on the monitor instead of your friend. Well, as I looked at the image of myself on my computer screen, I saw a shadowy figure lying on the bed behind me. I turned around and looked at the bed directly, but there was nothing there. I looked back at the monitor and saw the figure again, still lying there. It seemed to be gesturing as if it were saying something. I turned back to the bed again and I still couldn't see the figure, but I *did* see an indentation in the pillow *where its head would have been*. I walked over to the bed and put my hand in the area I thought the figure would be. The temperature was much colder there than in the rest of the room. When I went back to the monitor, I saw that everything was back to normal...the figure wasn't there anymore."

◆   ◆   ◆

Hal said that he's lived in several different places and often specu-
lates that the same spirit has followed him over the years to look after
him, though he's not certain.

"Whatever the case may be," Hal concluded, "I've never been afraid.
In fact, it comforts me to know that death is not the end."

*Was Hal correct in his assumption that he had a "guardian spirit" fol-
lowing him from place to place? Was there more than one ghost? And
were they simply checking up on Hal...or trying to communicate something to him? The answer may lie somewhere down the road, the next
time he encounters "la muerte"...*

Phantom Photographs

Eyewitness reports of ghost sightings are innumerable and, because of their very nature, are subject to either acceptance or dismissal by the recipient of such reports. When ghostly images appear on film, however, it's a little harder to discount them—especially for the photographer...

During my interview with Karen Gentry-Sizemore (*The Haunted Hotel*), she mentioned another oddity she had encountered earlier in her lifetime.

"Several years ago," Karen began, "my father had a friend named Herman that he worked with at the General Electric plant in Ohio. Dad was also acquainted with Herman's family; they weren't terribly close, but they were friends. Sadly, Herman passed away from what I believe was a heart attack.

"About a year after Herman passed away, his widow, along with their two daughters and two sons-in-law, went to the cemetery to visit his grave. It was Memorial Day, and Herman had been a World War II veteran. At some point during their visit, the family posed for a snapshot in front of the gravesite.

"After the film was developed, Herman's widow was looking at the pictures when she noticed something strange about one of them—the one that had been taken in front of Herman's grave. In the picture, she could see the vague outline of a human figure standing in front of the group—*it appeared to be Herman*. Although the image was faint, she could still make out the features well enough to tell that it was him.

"Oddly enough, the son-in-law that the figure appeared in front of was the one that Herman hadn't particularly cared for while he was alive. It was as if he were still trying to spite him from beyond the grave by trying to block him out of the picture. She showed the photo to her family and everyone agreed that it certainly appeared to be Herman.

"They thought they might somehow be imagining things, so the family visited their minister and showed *him* the photograph, saying nothing of what they had seen. Sure enough, the minister saw it too. He reassured them and said that it was just Herman's way of letting them know that he was okay…and that he still had a sense of humor.

"Eventually, Herman's widow showed the picture to my father. As before, she didn't mention what she and the others had seen. Now, my father is a very down-to-earth kind of guy who generally dismisses this sort of thing as nonsense, but when he saw the photograph, he immediately recognized the figure as his old friend Herman."

◆   ◆   ◆

I might mention that this is only one of many cases in which a ghostly image has been captured on film. There are many famous, documented cases of this type; more than likely, there are numerous more not-so-famous cases, most of which will probably remain unreported.

Perhaps the next time you're looking through a family photo album, you should pay close attention to those areas of the pictures that weren't the intended focal points—shadows, backgrounds, doorways and the like. Upon closer inspection, you may just discover that a long-passed member of your family has made an unexpected appearance…

The Discontented Ghost

Sometimes, when a family member passes on—especially if that person is particularly strong-willed or stubborn—he or she will somehow find a way to pierce the curtain between the spiritual and physical worlds and make an appearance to loved ones before permanently vanishing into the hereafter. The purpose of such an appearance might be to deliver a message, to ease someone's grief or—as the following story seems to indicate—to express a certain amount of discontent...

Vikki Whitman is a curriculum developer who works near my department. I paid her a visit not long ago and she shared with me a remarkable tale.

"My grandfather died in the summer of 1991," Vikki recalled. "His health had been failing for some time and he had been in a hospice for a couple of months when we finally decided to bring him home. During this time, I was staying at my grandmother's house in Chicago, helping out in whatever way I could. My aunts took turns during the day looking after Grandpa—bringing his meals, reading to him, things like that—and I was the 'midnight nurse'. He passed away about a week after we brought him home.

"I was still at Grandma's house on the night of the funeral. Late that night, I woke up and saw that the door to the right of my bed was open—it had been closed when I went to sleep. Then I noticed that *my grandfather was standing in the doorway!* I watched as he walked around to the far side of the bed. Needless to say, this scared the hell out of me. I thought I was having a really bad dream or something, so I pulled the covers up over my head. After I had worked up enough courage to peek out, he was gone and the door was closed again.

"The next morning, I was still a little freaked out, but I had basically shrugged the whole thing off as a dream—at least until my aunt came down for breakfast. The very first thing she said was, 'You'll never believe the dream I had last night...*Dad came and visited!*'"

Vikki proceeded to tell me that her aunt had experienced the same thing she had that night: Her father appeared in the doorway and walked around the bed in the same manner as he had in Vikki's room.

"I then told her about *my* experience," she added, "and we were both just floored. I later learned that, on the same night, my mom's other sisters had been calling the house with reports of strange goings-on. One of my aunts, who was keeping the urn at her house—my grandfather was cremated—said she had felt his presence in her room all night long. Another aunt told my mother that her empty clothes dryer kept coming on all night, and her TV kept turning on and off by itself."

It occurred to me at that point in the interview that Vikki's grandfather must have had quite a strong personality to be able to manifest his presence in so many ways and in so many different places on the same night.

"He *was* a very strong figure in the family," she admitted. "He was very stern, and a little cranky. But then again, he had seven children and I-don't-know-how-many grandchildren, so I guess he deserved to be cranky."

Vikki went on to say that, although she personally experienced no further occurrences after that night, her aunt continued to witness the same inexplicable activity with her clothes dryer and TV for months afterwards.

◆   ◆   ◆

Vikki concluded her story with an epilogue that seems to remove any doubt that her grandfather's spirit was indeed responsible for the strange happenings.

"Granddad used to frequent a certain farm in Indiana with his hunting buddies when I was growing up," she said. "He just loved it there. So, a few months after his death, the family took a road trip to the farm. We scattered his ashes there and hung a bird feeder in his name…that's where we visit him now. Since that day, there have been no further occurrences."

Perhaps the spirit of Vikki's grandfather was not content with the original location of his remains, and was somehow attempting to communicate his dissatisfaction through his funeral-night visitations and the strange activity of the appliances. Apparently, he succeeded. It seems likely that he would want his final resting place to be the spot at which he had spent so much time during his life—the beloved farm.

The Butterfly

*In the United States, there are those who believe in ghosts, those who
don't and those who are undecided. In certain other places, however,
there is a general consensus: Ghosts are real—though they may not
always appear in what Americans might consider "traditional form"…*

One of my colleagues, Jay Campbell, is a likeable fellow with a
knack for spinning a good yarn. One of his stories was of particular
interest to me.

"My wife is from a town in Northern Thailand called Chiang Rai,"
(pronounced "shang rye") Jay explained. "Ghosts are definitely a part
of the culture there. Unlike here in the 'States, there is no issue of belief
or disbelief—it's an accepted part of everyday life."

After a brief description of his journey to Thailand, how he came to
meet his wife, and his relationship with his in-laws, Jay continued.

"My brother-in-law had been educated in the Temple, which means
he had been a Monk. I guess he was probably there for about five or six
years, during which time he wore a bright, saffron-colored robe. Some
time later, he acquired the nickname 'Noi', which is sort of a respectful
nickname for someone who's been a Monk.

"After he left the temple, Noi went to Bangkok to find work. He
began having respiratory problems, but he wouldn't get help for it—he
just dismissed it as being a 'smoker's hack'. Well, by the time he finally
got medical attention and found out he had Tuberculosis, it was too
late. He died unexpectedly…*and* prematurely—he was only in his
early thirties."

◆   ◆   ◆

"During his life, Noi had shared a very close bond with his uncle, whose nickname happened to be 'Loong Noi'—'Loong' meaning 'Uncle' and 'Noi' because he had also been a Monk at one time. Loong Noi was fairly old—probably in his seventies—and was in poor health around the same time that Noi had been diagnosed with TB. Not the least of his ailments was a bad leg. His condition had gotten so bad that he had to be hospitalized by the time Noi had passed away.

"As I said before, the two had been very close. Well, on the morning that they brought Noi's body back to Chiang Rai from Bangkok, Loong Noi was visited in his hospital room by a butterfly, which flew in through the window and landed on his bad leg. The butterfly had *bright, saffron-colored wings.* At that very moment, Loong Noi passed away. My cousin-in-law—who was there at the time—and the people in the village believe that the butterfly was the spirit of Noi, coming to take his uncle away with him to the afterlife."

> *Even to a skeptic, this story would seem to demonstrate the capacity of the human spirit to prevail against physical affliction—even death—and rise above earthly bonds with beauty, grace, and quiet victory to reunite with a loved one. Clearly, this is a testament to the strength and immortality of family ties.*
>
> *There is one more aspect of this story that wraps it up rather poignantly: Three months after the passing of Noi and Loong Noi, as if to dispel any remaining doubts—or perhaps just to say one last good-bye—an abnormally large butterfly flew into the home of Jay's in-laws in Chiang Rai...you can probably guess what color its wings were...*

A Host of Ghosts

Sometimes, we may unwittingly invoke hauntings through the use of devices such as Ouija boards. There are those who believe the use of these instruments opens a "doorway" into the spirit world, which may stay open longer than the user intends—even after the board is put away—thus allowing the summoned entity or entities continued access to the physical world. Other hauntings seem to consist of deceased loved ones appearing briefly to comfort, help or perhaps just visit with their living family members. The following account seems to include both of these instances of spectral visitation...

One of the managers I work with, Yvonne Graham, caught me off guard one day when she admitted that *she* had a story I might find interesting. I stopped by her office after work that day, and she treated me to an intriguing tale.

"I lived in this house in Bedford (Texas) for three years—from '84 to '87," Yvonne began. "The area had some history to it in that there was an old creek that ran through it where travelers would sometimes camp, back in the 'olden days'. My daughter, who is very sensitive to the paranormal—you might even call her 'psychic'—told me once that she had the feeling someone had been killed there long ago. She believes that a young man was shot by his lover in that area, though I'm not sure if that has anything to do with what happened to us in the house.

"I don't recall exactly when the occurrences began, but I do remember that it was sometime after my father passed away. He died in January of '85, so I'm going to guess that these things started happening in the spring of that year.

"One night, I was asleep in my bed laying face down, when I woke up and felt something pushing me down into the bed. At first, I thought I was just having a bad dream. I was under a lot of stress at the time, so I didn't think much about it.

"A few nights later, it happened again. This time, it happened *before* I had fallen asleep. I could feel the same sensation of being pushed down into the bed, as if someone had placed one hand between my shoulder blades, and one on my legs, and was pressing down on me. I got the impression somehow that it was a *male*. At that point, I got up, stood in the middle of the room and shouted, *'I don't know who you are, but you need to leave me alone!'* I don't recall it happening again after that."

◆   ◆   ◆

"That summer, I went on vacation to Hawaii with a girlfriend of mine. On the return flight, there were complications with the aircraft, so we had to turn around and go back to Hawaii. My youngest son, Bruce—a senior in high school at the time—was staying at my house while I was gone.

"Bruce was expecting me back around seven o'clock that evening, so I called to let him know what was going on. While I was on the phone with him, I could tell by the tone of his voice that something was wrong, though he denied it at the time. Well, eventually, my girlfriend and I caught another flight out and made it home.

"A few nights later, Bruce finally admitted that there *had* been something amiss while I was gone. He came to me and said, 'You know, the strangest thing happened the other night while you were in Hawaii…' He went on to tell me that he had awakened that night and was having an insulin reaction—he was diabetic—so he went to the kitchen to get some orange juice or something. As he was standing there, he suddenly became very cold; he told me that he felt as if he were 'chilled to the bone'. He finished up in the kitchen and went back to bed with his juice. He said, 'It was so weird—I just felt a presence.' Later, he wound up closing the bedroom door and placing a foam rubber ball in front of it for some reason or another before going back to sleep.

"The next morning, he woke up to find that the ball was behind the bed and the bedroom door had been opened. When he walked out into the house, he saw that *every door in the house was standing wide open, and every drawer was pulled out!* Only the outside doors were still closed and locked. It was almost as if this presence or spirit was saying, *'I'm not going to hurt you...I'm just going to scare you to death.'*

"At some point during all of this, my mom spent the night with me. The next morning, as we were having coffee and reading the Sunday paper, I asked her how she had slept. She told me she'd had a very strange dream. She said she woke up and couldn't move, and that the bed was shaking violently. I just said, 'So I guess you've met Herman', which was kind of the nickname I'd given it."

At that point, Yvonne told me, she began thinking quite a bit about the mysterious goings-on and talking to friends in an effort to try and get to the bottom of things.

"I remembered that, at one time, a friend of mine and I had played around with a Ouija board there in the house. I thought that maybe our dabbling in the spirit world had somehow invited this unwanted presence into my home. So I found the Ouija board and put it out on the curb for the trash collectors to pick up. After that, I don't think there were any further occurrences."

◆   ◆   ◆

Yvonne related that nothing out of the ordinary happened for several years afterwards, but in the early '90s, a new batch of strange happenings started up.

"In 1992, my grandmother passed away," she said. "The following year, my aunt died. My son Bruce also passed away that year from complications with his diabetes. It was a traumatic couple of years for my mother and me; that was a lot to deal with in such a short period of time.

"In 1994, we moved into our current home. Incidentally, it's only about a block away from the house we moved out of. In the time since we moved into our new house, Mother has been visited by several of our loved ones who've passed on. She has seen her sister at the foot of her bed; she has also seen my son and my father. There's never any conversation…she just sees them standing there briefly. When she blinks or looks away for a moment, they disappear.

"She really doesn't feel threatened by any of this since, for the most part, she knows who the spirits are. But, quite often, she wakes up to what feels like someone *walking on her bed*. She describes it as feeling like a child has jumped up on the bed and is running around on it. Sometimes she feels as though someone is *under* the bed as well. Then there was the night she woke up and saw the figure of a dog sitting in her room—just sitting there, wagging its tail."

I asked Yvonne if her family had ever kept dogs in the house.

"My son had a dog at one time," she replied. "It was a black Labrador named 'Amos'. He died of old age. I suppose it's possible that the dog my mother saw that night could have been Amos.

"I believe that there's always someone waiting on 'the other side' for us, to help us through the transition of death. My fear is that this is why my mother is experiencing these nightly visitations, and I'm not ready for her to go."

◆　　◆　　◆

"In recent years, Bruce has made his presence known to us in different ways. During our move in '94, we had stuff scattered everywhere. Just before the move, my mother had placed her wedding rings in a little jewelry bag and had hidden them from the movers—and from herself, it turns out—just to be safe.

"Once we were settled into our new house, she searched high and low for the rings, but she couldn't find them. Then one day, as she was combing her hair in the bathroom, she said aloud, 'Bruce, you need to help me find my wedding rings.' Within thirty seconds, she had a strong urge to look in the drawer where she kept her bras. Sure enough, *the rings were there*. He helps her find things quite often.

"He can be kind of rowdy sometimes, too. He knocked a roaster pan onto the kitchen floor once…and he's turned on the TV quite a few times. My daughter says she 'feels' him a lot. We have no doubt that he's still around."

Did Yvonne and her friend unknowingly open a "doorway" through which the menacing spirit entered her home? Did this doorway remain open longer than expected? Is this also how her departed loved ones were able to make repeated appearances to Yvonne and her mother? And perhaps the most unsettling question of all: Is the doorway still open?

Home is Where the Haunt is

There is a theory among paranormal investigators that certain kinds of ghosts—known as "poltergeists"—are drawn to adolescents. The exact reason for this apparent fixation is not clear. Perhaps adolescent children emit more "psychic energy" than adults or younger children; perhaps the poltergeists feel awkward in their posthumous environment and find empathy in their living counterparts...

Probably my closest association with ghosts is my own sister, Ann. I remember hearing about many of her encounters just after they had happened, as we did, of course, grow up together in the same house.

Ann and I sat down to coffee recently and I asked her to recall the strange experiences she's had over the years.

"It started kind of slowly," she remembered. "The first noteworthy things happened when I was in my early teens. I would be sitting at the dining room table, doing homework, and I would feel someone standing very close behind me, as if they were looking over my shoulder. Of course, with that many people in the house, I just assumed that it was Mom or Dad, or one of you; but I would turn around and see that nobody was there. This happened quite often—once or twice a day.

"Then there were the times when I would be watching TV in the living room late at night, and I would hear the sounds of bare feet on the linoleum walking into the room and stopping behind the loveseat. Again, I always just thought it was one of you, coming in to see what I was watching. Of course, when I turned around, no one was there.

"That same linoleum was in the hallway. My bed was up against the wall that separated my room from the hall, with the door just a few feet away. Sometimes, as I lay in bed at night, I would hear the sounds of bare feet walking up and down the hallway—sometimes half the night, it seemed. So it started that way, with little things…mostly feelings and sounds."

◆   ◆   ◆

Ann and I agreed that, with some effort, weird sensations and strange noises can be explained away. But her experiences didn't stop there.

"The first time I actually *saw* something," she continued, "was one day when Mom brought me and some of my girlfriends home from school for lunch. We were having sandwiches and watching soap operas. At one point, I was standing in the kitchen, making myself a sandwich. With my peripheral vision, I saw a light-colored shape or figure come up the hallway and turn into the bathroom.

"I just assumed it was one of my friends, since I wasn't sure where each of them was at the time. It made me curious, though, because I hadn't seen any of them leave the living room. So I walked to the bathroom to see who it was, but no one was there.

"I searched the rest of the back rooms, but still didn't find anyone. When I returned to the living room, everyone was there, present and accounted for. But I just *knew* I had seen someone or something come up the hallway and turn into that room."

◆   ◆   ◆

If there *was* a ghost in the house that my sister and I grew up in, its activities apparently weren't limited to one particular area.

"A few of the occurrences took place in my bedroom," Ann remembered. "I had a chest of drawers with a large mirror on top of it across the room from my bed. I had been sleeping on my side facing the mirror one morning when Mom came in to wake me. As I opened a bleary eye, I could see her in the mirror, stooping over me. I could also make out a vague figure standing behind her. In the time it took me to close my eyes, register what I had seen and open them again, the figure was gone.

"Then there was the night I was laying in bed with my foot outstretched and I felt someone lay a hand on it. I guess you could say it was the blanket settling or something, but it was a much heavier feeling than that. And, as soon as I moved my foot, the feeling lifted. If it had been the blanket, that obviously wouldn't have happened.

"There was a time or two when I would be showering and, when I would reach for the towel, I'd find that it wasn't there. I'd peek through the shower curtain and see it a few feet away on the floor. If it had simply fallen off the rod, it would've been in a crumpled heap directly beneath the spot where I had hung it. But it wasn't. It was always a few feet away, as if it had been yanked off with a good deal of force.

"Then there was the day when you and Mom had gone to the grocery store and I was alone in the house, ironing school clothes in the dining room. My back was to the wall-mounted telephone we used to have there. As I stood there ironing, I caught a movement out of the corner of my eye. I turned around and saw the phone cord swinging back and forth, as if someone had stretched it out rubber band-style and let it go.

"Of course, I hadn't been using the phone and no one else was home, so I stood there looking at it for a few seconds, trying to make sense out of it. When I realized I couldn't, I went outside and waited for you and Mom to come home. That was really the first *tangible* thing that happened—the first thing that couldn't be explained away. That cord was swinging wildly for no apparent reason."

◆   ◆   ◆

Even at this point, one could doubt one's own senses and shrug off such occurrences as the results of an overactive imagination. But when *other* family members begin reporting similar incidents…well, that's a different story. I spoke with our mother to get *her* account of the events.

"Yes," she admitted, "I remember Ann telling me about these things that were happening, but I usually just played it down. I mean, what was I going to tell her? The stories she was telling didn't really surprise me because I'd had similar experiences, but I was fairly sure we weren't in any real danger."

I reviewed with Mom some of the incidents that Ann had described to me. Hearing each one, she nodded in remembrance. When I mentioned the story of Ann's awakening to see a figure standing behind her, she was quick to add her comments.

"That's not the first time someone has seen a figure standing behind me," she revealed. "One day while I was at work, I was standing near the register, talking to one of the ladies I work with. As I was talking to her, I noticed that she was not looking at me, but rather just *behind* me. I asked her what she was looking at and she said, *'There's a man standing behind you.'* I turned around, but didn't see anybody. Then she said, 'Yes…he has a hat on.' A few seconds later, she told me that he was gone.

"From the way she described the man, he sounded very much like my uncle, who died many, many years ago. I was only six or seven years old when he passed away, but I remember him always being very protective of me."

◆   ◆   ◆

During the interview with my sister, she had alluded to an incident that happened when our mother was at the house by herself. I asked Mom about this.

"Yes, I had just come home from grocery shopping one afternoon," she recalled. "Your father was at work and you kids were in school, so the house was empty…or so I thought. I went in through the carport door—like I always do—and I was standing in the kitchen when I heard a cough, then a voice, coming from somewhere in the back of the house. It scared me badly.

"I went out the front door and stood there, wondering what to do. I was afraid to go back in, so I walked across the street and got our neighbor, Alan. I kept my eye on the house the whole time, in case anyone came out. Alan grabbed his gun and we both went back over to the house. He had me wait outside while he went in and searched the house. He looked everywhere, but couldn't find anyone. Then I went in and we made a second pass through the house, together. We looked in closets, under beds, everywhere…but we found nothing.

"As you know, there are only three doors going into the house—the front door, the back door and the carport door. Like I said, I kept my eyes on the house the whole time I was getting Alan, so nobody could have come out of the front or side door without me seeing them. We found that the back door was still locked from the inside. No one could've gotten out through a window, because we had all our windows secured with screws."

I asked Mom to describe exactly what she had heard.

"It was a male voice," she said. "If I stopped and thought about it hard enough, I could probably remember what the voice said. It was only a couple of words, but it really scared me. Well, the *cough* scared me…but then I heard the voice, and I just *had* to get out of there. I don't know exactly what the voice was saying, but I think it was of a menacing nature, because that's what I sensed."

◆   ◆   ◆

Mom went on to describe some other strange occurrences she's experienced throughout her life.

"I've been in certain places where I've had these…feelings," she confided. "It's kind of hard to describe. There have been times when I've sensed a presence in my house, but it wasn't a menacing presence; it was more of a *comforting* presence. I think if you're open to that kind of thing, you can pretty much sense whether it's good or bad.

"There's *definitely* a presence in the house your father grew up in, in West Virginia. It's kind of borderline menacing; it makes me a little afraid, but mostly it makes me extremely sad, to the point that I actually feel like crying. Being there makes me very uncomfortable—I just want to get out of there. I have to really put on an act when I'm in that house to keep myself in the present moment, and not just let the feeling overwhelm me. And don't even *think* about trying to get me to go down into the basement."

I asked Mom if my grandfather had built the house, or if it had a previous occupant.

"I doubt that he built it," she replied. "I know he did a lot of things to it after he bought it, but I don't think he was the original owner."

I speculated that the presence in the house might have stemmed from something that had happened there before my grandfather moved his family into it.

"That could have been it," she supposed. "Or it could have been your father's stepmother—who was the typical 'wicked stepmother'—because she died in that house. I found this out *after* spending the night there once. They told me that I had slept in the room she had died in…and in the very *bed* she'd died in. I told your father that if he ever wants me to go to West Virginia with him again, we'll have to get a motel room, because I won't stay in that house again.

"Now, I should mention that, when I visited the *second* of the two houses your father had lived in as a boy, I felt nothing unusual at all. But at the *other* house…you can feel the dread even as you're pulling into the driveway."

Mom recalled another occasion, years earlier, when my father took her to visit his aunt, who also lived in West Virginia.

"That place was just plain *scary*," she recalled. "I'll never go back into *that* house either—morning, noon or night. It was a two-story house, typical of the ones in that area, with a big porch and a screen door leading inside. We walked up onto the porch where your father's aunt was sitting and sat down in the swing. The whole time we were sitting there, I was feeling very uncomfortable, although I had no idea why.

"After we talked on the porch for a while, your dad said something along the lines of, 'Let's go inside and look at the pictures.' I didn't say anything, but I was thinking, *'I really don't want to go in there...'* So we went inside...and *that* was worse than being on the porch. But when we started up the stairs to the bedroom, the feeling got so bad that I actually turned around, walked back down the stairs, and went back out onto the porch. I just couldn't stay inside that house any longer.

"At the time, I never thought about a *presence* being there...I just thought the *house* was making me feel that way. It really scared me, because I had never experienced anything like that before."

◆   ◆   ◆

Ann and I have long since moved out of the house we grew up in, though our parents still live there today. Many years have passed since the aforementioned occurrences took place, but whatever entity was responsible for them still seems to be hanging around, as my sister attested near the close of our chat.

"I went back for a visit not too long ago," Ann explained. "I stayed in my old room, which is now Mom's room. That night, as I was lying in bed, I suddenly felt like somebody was standing next to the bed. It was quite a strong feeling. I opened my eyes and didn't see anything, so I tried to talk myself out of being scared, attributing my uneasiness to things that had happened there in the past.

"I flopped over on my back and was lying there with my eyes open. Out of the corner of my eye, I saw a dark shape move across the front of the mirror that hung on the wall opposite the bed. That's when I said, 'enough of this', and went into the other room to wake up Mom so she could sleep with me.

"That's a pretty pathetic thing for a 30-year-old to do, but I wasn't about to lie in there all night by myself. Besides, it (the ghost) seems to like Mom. In fact, I kind of had the feeling that maybe it thought *I* was *her*, and it was just checking in on her or something. I had this sense that it was kind of surprised to see somebody other than Mom in that bed."

Growing up with a ghost in the house doesn't seem to have had any lasting negative effects on my sister—with the possible exception of a bit of uneasiness during overnight stays with our parents (even I can't help casting a nervous glance about the guest room before dozing off when I'm visiting there). Our mother doesn't seem to mind sharing the house with the seemingly friendly spirit (or spirits), either. As long as the "coughing ghost" doesn't return, she says, everything will be just fine…

Cemetery Visitor

As we've examined previously, strange apparitions can sometimes be attributed to overactive imaginations—especially where children are concerned. But how do you explain a mysterious vision witnessed by seven children at the same time?

Lou Ann Gross, a scriptwriter for our video department, is the quintessential extrovert, always ready for a bit of impromptu socialization. One of my occasional visits to her cubicle yielded quite an interesting story.

"I grew up in Raleigh, North Carolina," Lou Ann told me. "We lived in a neighborhood built on what was once the site of an old plantation. The neighborhood was called 'Carriage Hills', probably as a tribute to the old plantation and the carriages that people used to ride through that area. Back in the 1800s, when the farming families lived there, they planted rows and rows of crops. It's evident even today in the contour of the land and the way the trees grow there.

"There was this old cemetery in our neighborhood—it was the only thing left from the plantation days. I suppose it was left alone out of respect...or superstition. Whatever the reason, it was left standing, and the houses in my neighborhood were actually built *around* it.

"The cemetery was up on this big hill and there was a huge magnolia tree in the middle of it. There were probably 30-some-odd tombstones there, some of which were quite large and impressive. Judging from the names on the headstones, there must've been about seven or eight farming families that lived in that area and buried their dead there. I remember the most recent date on the headstones being in the mid-1950s. Most of them were much older, of course.

"There were probably about fourteen kids in our neighborhood when I was growing up. We were all pretty close to the same age—seven, eight or nine years old. Now, this may sound strange, but that cemetery was kind of like our playground. We'd climb up in that big magnolia tree and we'd make little roads in the red clay dirt to drive our little toy cars on. We didn't really think of it as a 'scary' place…it was just a place where we hung out and played.

"These days, that neighborhood is fairly urbanized, but back then it was pretty well secluded—you never saw any strangers passing through. Well, one day while we were playing in the cemetery—there were probably about seven of us there, my brother included—several of us looked up and saw this man walking up the street toward us. He was very tall and gangly and he wore an old-fashioned hat and a long frock coat. We were all a little scared because we were quite young and here was this strange man in our neighborhood.

"Now, I should tell you that there was a correctional facility about five miles away, and inmates would escape from time to time, occasionally ending up in our neighborhood. This was our first assumption. But the clothes that the man was wearing didn't make sense to us; even as young as we were, we knew that his clothes were out of place in that day and age.

"Well, by that time, the man had gotten closer. He was only about fifty feet up the road from us—close enough for us to make out his features fairly well. We all looked at each other with these 'who-the-heck-is-that' expressions and, when we turned around again, *he was gone*. Of course, being so young and simple-minded, we just kind of shrugged it off and went back to our playing.

"I've thought about it over the years, trying to make sense of it. There were woods nearby that the man could have run into, but he would have had to move *very* quickly in that short amount of time. Besides—why would he suddenly run into the woods? Also, there was a little hill that separated the road from the trees…surely we would have seen him going up that hill. And what about those old-fashioned clothes? The whole thing was just bizarre. It's the kind of thing that just sticks with you...it's still very, very vivid in my mind."

◆　　◆　　◆

After a bit of speculative conversation about the "tall stranger" incident, Lou Ann went on to tell me about a *second* occurrence that took place at the cemetery, years later.

"When I was fourteen," she recalled, "I used to jog around the neighborhood every day after school. One afternoon, as I was jogging past the cemetery, I suddenly found that I couldn't move. It was as if some invisible force had *grabbed* me; I just couldn't take another step. So I freaked out and started screaming, but I don't think anyone heard me. Well, after about fifteen seconds, whatever it was that had me suddenly let go. I took off and ran back to my house to wait until my mother got home."

Lou Ann expressed that if she'd had any lingering doubts about the authenticity of her childhood encounter at the cemetery, they were permanently dispersed by the jogging incident.

"I'm not terribly surprised that I had those visions or experiences," she concluded. "Of all the kids in my neighborhood, I was the only one who was ever really concerned about the upkeep of the cemetery...and probably the only one who ever wondered about the people who were buried there."

> *Who was the strange figure in the old-fashioned clothing that Lou Ann and her childhood friends saw in the cemetery that day? Was it the ghost of a former plantation owner, taking a leisurely stroll on what was once his property? Was he one of the many who were laid to rest in the cemetery decades before? Lou Ann has no explanations...only the vivid and persistent memories of what she experienced there years ago...*

In the Wee, Small Hours

Some people seem born to shine, to touch the lives of others, to enter-
tain. Their main purpose, it seems, is to inject friendship, consolation
or humor into the empty spaces in our lives. Often, these people are pos-
sessed of such effervescence that they are subconsciously and unwittingly
perceived by those around them to be more or less invincible, for the
thought of such liveliness ceasing to exist is incomprehensible to most. If
the following story is any indication, perhaps the subconscious is onto
something...

My part-time coworker and good friend Lisa Collins is a wife and
mother of three who somehow still manages to find time occasionally
to pursue her interest in community theater. Lisa has many anecdotes
from her days of heavier involvement in theatrical productions, one of
which just happens to be perfectly suited for this book.

"This happened during the summer of 1994," Lisa began. "I was a
newlywed, living in a new house, and life was great. I spent most of my
free time rehearsing for a Broadway revue charity show in the community theater circuit. This was the third show I had done, and I had
become very close to the group of people who were working on it.

"We loved each other like family, and we spent as much time
together as possible. The revues were what brought us together, but
there were several other factors that really cemented our relationships.
We shared births, weddings and breakups—things like that. But I
think the saddest thing we ever went through together was the loss of
one of our fellow performers, Paul.

"Paul was an extremely talented singer and dancer. He had a wry,
sardonic sense of humor and a knack for making you laugh when the
stress level got really high. He was also the type of person that cared

deeply for the people he was close to, but he wasn't always able to show it. Paul performed with us during our first two shows, but he became very ill and wasn't able to join us for the third one.

"On the opening night of our third show, Paul's partner came into the dressing room and told us that Paul had lost his battle with AIDS and had died that afternoon. There were thirty of us in the cast, and all of us knew and loved Paul. Our first reaction was to cancel that evening's performance, but after we discussed it for a few minutes, we decided to go on with the show. Paul would have wanted it that way.

"We dedicated that evening's show and the rest of the shows to Paul. In honor of his memory, we changed our benefiting charity to an AIDS research-related foundation. During the run, when I was backstage waiting for an entrance, I would sometimes catch glimpses of Paul out of the corner of my eye, in the dimly-lit recesses of the wings. I would turn and look more closely and realize it was actually someone else standing across the stage, or a coat rack, or some other stage dressing. I guess it was just my desire to see him one more time, causing my mind to play tricks on me."

◆   ◆   ◆

"About six weeks after the show closed, our group got together to attend the opening night of the Disney movie, *The Lion King*. After the movie, we all congregated at my house to talk, have a few drinks and listen to music. I had recently bought a copy of the soundtrack from *Sleepless in Seattle* and it was one of my favorites at the time, so I played it for everyone.

"One of the songs on that CD is called *In The Wee, Small Hours Of The Morning*. It had reminded me of Paul ever since I first heard it. The verse that made me think of him goes like this:

In the wee, small hours of the morning,
While the whole wide world is fast asleep,
You lie awake and think about the boy

And never ever think of counting sheep.
When your lonely heart has learned its lesson,
You'd be his if only he'd call;
In the wee, small hours of the morning—
That's the time you miss him most of all.

"I think it reminded me of Paul because, after he died, I spent many nights lying awake and thinking about him. It made me so angry that a terrible disease like AIDS could take the life of someone with so much talent and promise. It always made me incredibly sad, too. Those nights…they really *were* the times I missed him most of all.

"Paul's partner was with us on the night of our get-together after *The Lion King*. It was the first night he'd been out since Paul passed away, and it meant a lot to us to have him there. The conversation never turned specifically to Paul, but he was on everyone's mind.

"After the party broke up, I stayed up for quite a while longer, listening to music and thinking of the evening and of Paul. My husband was out of town at the time, so I was alone in the house. After a while, I turned off the stereo and all the lights and went to bed.

"Much later—in the wee, small hours of the morning—I had a dream that I was again with the group from the show, and the *Sleepless in Seattle* soundtrack was playing softly in the background. The song that was playing in my dream was, of course, *In The Wee, Small Hours Of The Morning*. It was one of those moments when you're half-asleep and not really sure if you're dreaming, or what. I specifically remember feeling that way and thinking that if the next song on the CD played, I would know I wasn't dreaming. The next song on the CD lineup was the old Roy Rogers tune, *Back In The Saddle Again*.

"So I laid there still half-asleep as the song finished and, sure enough, I heard the opening strains of *Back In The Saddle Again*. At that point, I realized I *wasn't* dreaming and I sat bolt upright in bed. I just sat there for a few seconds, thinking, *'Who turned on the CD player?'* I walked into the living room and found that the stereo was in fact on and was playing that CD.

"Of course, I wondered if I had inadvertently left the stereo on...but I specifically remember turning it off. Besides, our CD player isn't the kind that automatically starts over when the last song has played. Even if it were, the two songs I'd heard were right in the *middle* of the CD, so *why hadn't I heard the songs that came before them?*

"The only conclusion I can draw is that Paul was there that night and was sending me a message that he knew I was thinking of him. I'm not sure *why* he was there—maybe his partner's presence drew him to us—but I definitely sensed him in my house for the rest of that night. I haven't felt his presence since then...but in the wee, small hours of the morning—that's still the time I miss him most of all."

How can one explain a stereo that turns itself on in the middle of the night to play the requiem for a recently deceased friend? As Lisa describes him, Paul was a born performer; perhaps he couldn't resist coming back that night for one final encore...

The Waving Woman

Some ghosts seem to have "habits"—things they do each time they're witnessed. This would seem to give us clues as to what kind of people they were while living, or perhaps under what circumstances they may have died. Our next tale involves just such a habitual spirit...

The facility at which I work includes an exercise room where employees can get in a quick workout on their lunch breaks. During one such workout, I ran into Jeannie Hernandez, who works across the hall from me. Our ensuing conversation yielded an intriguing story from Jeannie's past.

"When I was a sophomore in high school," she explained, "my family was living in the Woodlawn Lake area of west central San Antonio. The house we were living in was built in the early 1900s, and had some historical significance, but I don't recall exactly what it was. Our family constantly rented, and this was just one of the houses we stayed in for a while.

"The house had kind of an unusual layout. There were two front doors leading inside from the front porch. One of the doors led into the living room and the other one led into the bedroom that my sister and I shared. On the other side of our bedroom was a door that led into the hallway. Our hallway ran past the bathroom and into my parents' bedroom. It was only a two-bedroom house.

"One night, my parents were in bed watching TV. My dad was facing the door that led into the hallway. At one point, he grabbed my mom's arm; she looked at him and saw that he was as white as a sheet. She asked him what was wrong, and he said, *'Who's that lady in the hallway, waving at us?'* He turned to my mother and, when he turned back, the woman in the hallway was gone. He explained it away as having been just a shadow, or the light from the TV causing him to see things.

"On another night, a few weeks later, my sister was in the bathroom when she saw the door opening slowly. She peeked into the hallway and saw the same thing my father had seen—the figure of a woman, waving at her. In describing the woman, my dad and sister have told me that she really had no distinct features; they just saw this vague, whitish figure of a woman."

◆   ◆   ◆

Up to that point, Jeannie admitted, she hadn't personally experienced anything out of the ordinary. But that would soon change.

"As I said before," she continued, "my sister and I shared a bedroom in the front part of the house. It had two windows that looked out onto the porch. Well, I woke up early one morning after a restless night and was telling my sister about the nightmare I'd had. In my dream, there were babies crying outside our bedroom window. Her eyes got really big, and she told me that *she'd had the very same dream*.

"Of course, this freaked us out. We figured that there must have been some cats fighting outside the window that night, although there weren't any wild or stray cats in our neighborhood. About a month later, it happened *again*—we woke up one morning to find that we'd both dreamt about babies crying on the porch, outside our window."

Jeannie informed me that the porch ran the width of the house and extended out about eight feet from the structure. I wondered if, at one time, it might have been screened in or enclosed and used as a nursery area.

"I have no knowledge of the house prior to our moving in, but I suppose it's possible," she speculated.

◆   ◆   ◆

"I don't recall anything happening until almost a year after we'd had those dreams," Jeannie continued. "My friend Viola and I were in the high school band, so we had to leave for school very early in the morning for band practice. Usually, Viola and her mother would come by my house around 5:45 or so to pick me up.

"One morning, as I was coming down the walk to the driveway, I noticed that Viola's mom was waving from the car, so I waved back. When I got into the car, she was kind of laughing and said, 'I wasn't waving at you, I was waving at your grandmother.' I told her that my grandmother didn't live with us, and that everyone was still asleep. She said, *'Then who was that lady waving at me from your bedroom doorway?'* At that point, I knew something strange was going on. I knew she hadn't seen my sister—who was in the shower at the time—and she said that the woman she'd seen was an *older* woman, which is why she assumed it was my grandmother.

"My sister had an early swim class with her friends, so she would leave the house shortly after I did. One morning, as she was climbing into the car with her friends, they asked who the lady was that had just been waving to them. My sister knew that I had already left the house and that everyone else was asleep, so she knew it must have been the ghost. That was the last of the sightings...we moved out of the house shortly after that."

In closing, Jeannie made some observations about the strange goings-on in the house.

"It's funny," she reflected, "the figure of the woman was only seen either late at night or very early in the morning...but I never did see her myself. I still have dreams about that house for some reason, though. There was quite a bit of turbulence in our household during that period—difficulties our family was going through. Maybe *that* somehow prompted the ghostly activities."

Who was the mysterious waving woman? Apparently, she was a friendly sort, possibly just checking in on Jeannie and her family from time to time in the midst of their difficulties. And what about the crying babies? Were they somehow connected with the woman? It's doubtful we'll ever know. But I can't help wondering—when Jeannie and her family packed up their things to move on to another rental house, was there a figure in the window waving goodbye as they drove away?

The Thing in the Cabin

Hauntings aren't always comprised of tangible elements. Granted, apparitions, unexplained noises and inexplicable happenings are probably the most common forms of ghostly manifestation, but sometimes hauntings occur in the form of mere feelings—an almost palpable sense of an unseen presence.

While they may be somewhat less popular than "mainstream" hauntings, these encounters of the non-tactile variety should not be regarded as any less significant. As we'll examine in this next story, sometimes what we feel can be far more frightening than what we see or hear...

A few years ago, my sister Ann and her husband Scott decided to take a bit of a vacation to the little town of Joseph, Oregon. It was during this trip that she had what she describes as the most terrifying experience of her life. She told me this story for the first time immediately upon returning from the trip and has retold it on a few occasions since. Recently, I visited with her in order to get the full account.

"We chose Oregon because we thought it would be nice to get away for a little while and see that part of the country," she began. "I checked out some travel guides from the library to get some ideas on where to go, what to do, and where to stay during our trip. One of the guides advertised a little town called Joseph, and a little grouping of cabins that could be rented up there by the lake.

"When I called to see about reserving a cabin, I was informed that they were all booked up at that time, except for one. I asked about it, and was given the run-down on the cabin's amenities, rental fees, etc. It sounded okay, so I went ahead and booked it for five nights. A few weeks later, Scott and I were on our way to Oregon."

◆   ◆   ◆

"We arrived at the cabin about mid-afternoon, after flying into a nearby town and then making the four-hour drive from the airport. The cabin was a two-story arrangement, with access to the second floor through a trap door in the ceiling, obviously at the top of a set of steps. The first floor consisted of a living area with a fold-out couch, a fireplace and a bathroom. The bedroom was upstairs, along with a much smaller room that contained only a tiny bed and a dresser.

"One of the first things we noticed about the place was the unusual placement of some of the inside door locks. Under the stairs, there was a door to what we assumed was a closet or small storage area. We noticed that it had a lock on the outside, which struck us as odd. Scott guessed that the door might not hang evenly on its hinges, and that the lock was there to keep it from swinging open on its own. We tried it out and found that this wasn't the case—the door stayed closed without the lock. Upstairs, the door that separated the bedroom from the smaller room had the same type of lock on it—again, on the outside. We couldn't figure this out, but we shrugged it off.

"I didn't really think about it at the time, but I felt a little uneasy about the cabin as soon as we arrived. The style of the place wasn't exactly up-to-date, so I guess I just attributed my uneasiness to the unfamiliar surroundings and the unsavory decor.

"After we had given the place a once-over, Scott left to drive to the local market for food and supplies. I was tired and wasn't feeling very well, so I stayed behind and took a little nap on the couch that was underneath the steps. As I drifted off to sleep, I had the strange feeling that I was being watched from above. A little while later, Scott returned and we left the cabin together to do some sightseeing.

"By the time we got back to the cabin that evening, we were both pretty tired, so we decided to shower and call it a night. I showered first, then went upstairs to turn down the bedspread and get ready for bed while Scott took his turn washing up.

"As I stood up there waiting for Scott to finish up, I began feeling increasingly uncomfortable in that room. I couldn't quite put my finger on it, but there was *something* not right about it. By the time Scott finally came upstairs, the feeling had gotten so strong that I suggested we sleep downstairs on the foldout couch. He asked me why, and I said, 'I don't know, I just don't want to stay up here.' Of course, he thought the idea was ridiculous, and said, 'Oh, come on, let's just sleep up here—this bed is comfortable.' With that, he turned out the light and we got into bed.

"I slid over as close as I could get to him, all the while feeling more and more apprehensive. We hadn't been there for more than two or three minutes when the feeling came over me that if I didn't get out of that room immediately, something was literally *going to get me*. It almost seemed like there was something *hovering over the bed*. I jumped up and ran down the stairs as fast as I could. As I stood at the bottom of the steps, I could see the light come on upstairs and Scott's feet stumbling around as he gathered up the pillows and sheets, wondering what the hell was going on.

"As I stood there watching him, I remember thinking, *'Hurry, hurry, hurry!'* At that point, I was not only afraid for myself, but for Scott as well. I felt like whatever it was up there was going to get *him* too if he didn't hurry up and get out of there. He finally came down, and I said, 'Close the door,' referring to the trap door. He asked me why, and I said, *'Just close the door!'* He closed it.

"Once we were both downstairs and the trap door was shut, Scott asked me what had happened. I was freaking out pretty badly by then, but I felt that whatever was up there had been 'sealed off'—I didn't feel that it had followed us downstairs. I was still on edge, though, because I knew that it was still within close proximity of us.

"I felt this kind of 'rushing' sensation in my head, almost as if I were *feeling* something that had happened there before. I had an image of a woman's face in my mind; she had dark hair and her mouth was open as if she were screaming. I was so scared and out-of-sorts that I was almost hysterical.

"Scott was trying desperately to get me to tell him what was wrong. He was asking, 'What? Did you see something? What did you see?' I said, 'No, but there's something bad up there.' He asked me, 'Up where?' I said, 'Up *there*,' and I pointed to the ceiling.

"Without realizing it, I was pointing directly at the location of the tiny little room upstairs. In retrospect, I'm sure that little room was the source of…whatever it was. But I just kept repeating, *'There's something bad up there…there's something bad up there…'* It was so strange—those words were just coming out of my mouth without me realizing that I was saying them.

"By this time, Scott was starting to get freaked out, too, because of the way I was acting. I'm not what you would call easily frightened, but at that moment, I was scared stiff—so much so that I was crying. I've never been that scared before in my life. Every hair on my body was literally standing on end.

"It took me about an hour to calm down. In fact, I was putting my things back in my suitcase and getting ready to leave, even though we were out in the middle of nowhere and had no place else to go. Scott even asked me if I wanted to sleep out in the car, but it was too cold out that night. After I had calmed down quite a bit and was thinking more clearly, I realized that we had no place to go. We had to stay there for the night.

"I had Scott drag the foldout couch as far from the trapdoor as he could get it, and we left all the lights on. He dozed off about ten or fifteen minutes later, but I stayed awake most of the night—I was still too scared to go to sleep. Eventually, though, exhaustion got the best of me, and I fell asleep too."

◆   ◆   ◆

"The next morning, I was feeling more than a little stupid for behaving the way I had. I decided not to leave just yet. I figured I had just overreacted or something. Besides, we had already paid for five nights there. So that day, we did some sightseeing, some hiking and some other 'touristy' things like that.

"Occasionally, we had to go back to the cabin for one reason or another. Even in the light of day, I was afraid to go in there. When I had to go to the bathroom, I would leave the door partially open and have Scott stand right outside. When I showered that night, I had him stand *in the room* with me. I wouldn't let him go upstairs for *any* reason. And, of course, there was no way *I* was going up there again, either. The trap door was kept closed. We slept on the foldout couch again that night…and again, with all the lights on.

"On the third day, we decided to go ahead and leave. We were feeling a little braver during those last moments, so we decided to try and get some pictures of the upstairs bedroom before we left—we had already done some videotaping downstairs the previous evening with a video camera we had borrowed from a friend. Scott went up the steps first, and managed to talk me into coming up just for a minute. We snapped off a few photos and left.

"It was a tremendous relief to finally get out of there. It was a funny thing, though—as we were checking out, the lady at the office didn't seem the least bit surprised that we were leaving two days early. She didn't ask the obvious questions you'd think someone in her position would ask, such as, 'Is there anything wrong?' or, 'Are you not enjoying your stay?' or anything along those lines. Nothing."

Ann and I agreed that the apparent nonchalance of the office attendant regarding their premature checkout would seem to indicate that hasty departures from that particular cabin were fairly commonplace.

I asked her about the pictures they had taken at the cabin.

"The photos really didn't show anything out of the ordinary," she said, "but there *was* something strange about the video footage we'd shot. When we played it back, we noticed that any time we had gotten near the staircase or the trap door, the camera would go black or the footage would become distorted."

◆   ◆   ◆

Having left the cabin hundreds of miles behind her, it would seem that the ordeal was over for Ann. *Or was it?*

"Soon after we got home," she remembered, "I started having nightmares about the cabin—at least three nights a week, it seemed. The dream differed a little each time I had it, but the general premise was always the same: I was back at the cabin in the upstairs bedroom with the 'thing'. Scott was working the graveyard shift at the time, so I was alone at night.

"Each time I had this dream, I had the odd sensation that the 'thing' was trying to *come through* my dream and into the apartment where I was. I would always note the time after waking up from these nightmares; it was always around 3:00 a.m. From what I'd heard, that's the time when most paranormal activity occurs. It wasn't very reassuring to wake up alone after a nightmare like that and see the clock showing 3:00 a.m.

"In addition to the nightmares, strange things started happening in my apartment. Things would disappear. I had so many hand towels vanish on me that I started accusing Scott of taking them to use at work, or washing his truck with them. He assured me that he hadn't taken any. I lost so many towels that I eventually had to buy more.

"Objects were also misplaced around the apartment. I would look for something and not be able to find it. Then, a few days later, it would turn up in a place I was certain I hadn't put it.

"I was hearing a lot of 'knocking' sounds, also. At first, I thought they were just normal apartment noises, coming from one of the units near mine. But, before long, I realized that it was coming from *inside* my apartment. This really put me off, because I'd always heard that knocking noises were indicative of 'bad spirits'.

"There were a few nights when I'd be laying in bed and I would hear a rapping sound on the wall right next to my ear, which startled me, to say the least. Then there were times when I'd be sitting in the living room and I'd hear knocking on the wooden dining room table—three sharp knocks.

"There were other noises as well. One night, as I was straightening up the books on the coffee table, I heard the distinct jingling sound of a set of keys coming from directly behind me. I turned around and saw that there was nothing there. Then there was the morning I was awakened very early by the sound of the metallic Venetian blinds in the dining room crinkling, as if someone were pushing them aside. I thought for sure that someone was breaking into my apartment. My cat, Boo, was lying next to me, so I knew it wasn't him. Scott was still at work, so I was alone. I grabbed the shotgun that we kept next to the bed and I started toward the dining room, still hearing the crinkling of the blinds. I rounded the corner and was surprised—and relieved—to find nobody there. I turned on the light and checked for any possible cause for the noise, but I found nothing.

"There were also times when I felt as if I wasn't alone. I would be lying in bed at night with my cat, and he would suddenly become alert. He would stare toward the bedroom door and down the hallway as if he were seeing something I couldn't. While this was happening, I would usually hear the scuffling sound of feet on the carpet, and I'd have the sense of a presence in the room with me. I might have been able to blow it off as my imagination, but the cat would perk up and listen and look at the same time I was hearing and feeling these things.

"I would sometimes catch Boo watching something—his eyes would be tracking something I couldn't see. One night, I was standing near the kitchen, holding him propped up against my shoulder. My back was to the hallway and he was facing it. I was just standing there petting him when I felt him tense up, so I pulled him away from me far enough to see his little face. He had his eyes fixed intently on something in the hallway. I stood there and watched his face as he tracked something that, judging from the movement of his eyes, walked up the hallway and stopped *right behind me*. That was very unnerving."

◆   ◆   ◆

"This whole situation reached a climax one night, a little over a year after it had started. I was having the same nightmare, only this time it was much more realistic than it had been before. As I was waking up from the dream, I remember hearing myself saying aloud, *'It's come through! It's come through!'* I still recall being so frightened as I was waking up that I was curled up in a fetal position, and I literally 'wanted my mom', as a child would. It was the most frightened I had been from the nightmares.

"As before, the clock showed 3:00 a.m. I sat up and tried to calm down, repeating to myself that it was just a dream. I would usually just roll over and go back to sleep after having the dream, but on this particular morning, I couldn't shake the feeling. So I got up and took the cat with me into the kitchen to get a drink of water, turning on lights as I went. Still, I couldn't shake the feeling; I felt as if the 'thing' had *succeeded* in coming through my dream, and was *in my bedroom*.

"I went into the living room and turned on the TV for a while. But the feeling persisted, even growing a little stronger. I tried to call Scott, but I couldn't get hold of him. That's when I called you. You weren't much help, because you were half asleep, of course—it *was* four o'clock in the morning.

"After I hung up the phone, I picked up Grandma's Bible, which I kept on the coffee table. I started saying the Lord's Prayer over and over, and asking God to protect me from whatever was in my bedroom. I just sat there on the couch with the Bible and waited and waited. Eventually, the sun came up, my fear subsided and that was the end of it—the nightmares stopped, the strange occurrences stopped, the cat stopped acting funny—it all just sort of quit after that morning."

What was the unseen presence in the cabin's upstairs bedroom? What had happened there? How many other unwary travelers have experienced the terror of the thing in the cabin? Did it actually succeed in coming through Ann's dream? Has it returned to the cabin? There's only one way to find out, I suppose—take a little trip to Joseph, Oregon, and rent it for yourself. You'll probably find that it's the only one available...

In the Back Bedroom

Childhood is a time of magic, vulnerability and wide-eyed innocence. More often than not, it's the only time in a person's life when he or she is completely open-minded. Perhaps this early state of naiveté allows children to perceive things that go largely unnoticed by adults; perhaps it even draws these "things" to the children…

Laura Hatch, one of the more recent transfers to my workplace, is from Boston, Massachusetts. While chatting with Laura one day about the house she grew up in, I realized that the Parker House Hotel isn't the only haunted structure in that region.

"This happened in a town just north of Boston, called 'Lynn'," Laura explained. "The house I grew up in was an older house—built in 1904. I guess the best way to describe the style would be 'Colonial'. The layout of the house was similar to others in that area, with the living room, dining room and kitchen downstairs and the bedrooms upstairs. The house also had a basement and an attic.

"My family moved into this house when I was three. My mother assigned a small bedroom, way off in the back of the house, to me. It was a very small room, barely big enough for a twin bed and a bureau. Looking back, I don't think it was intended to be a bedroom when it was built—maybe a sewing room or something, but not a bedroom.

"Soon after we moved into this house, I began to constantly talk to my mother about an 'invisible friend' in my room. I would describe his skin tone, hair color and clothes…just very vivid details of this man. I even drew pictures of him. This constant talk about my 'special friend' made my mother nervous, because she herself had seen 'shadows' moving through the house on occasion. My stepfather worked odd shifts during that time, so my mother was sometimes alone in the house at night."

◆   ◆   ◆

Laura went on to say that she occupied the tiny room for four years, until her younger sister Kristen was born.

"At that time," Laura continued, "I moved out of the room and Kristen moved in, inheriting the meager furnishings along with it. Well, after I had moved out, my vivid recollections and talk of my 'special friend' stopped. But, during *her* stay in the room, Kristen never slept well; she just couldn't seem to sleep in there, for some reason. Then, when my sister Jessica was born about four years later, my mother decided not to put her in the little room because of what had happened to me and to Kristen."

◆   ◆   ◆

One might think that a long period of dormancy would rid such a room of any unwanted entities. As Laura revealed, however, this was not the case.

"After another four or five years had passed," she said, "my youngest sister, Stacey, was born. I guess my mother's mind had eased by that time, because she decided to put Stacey in that same tiny back bedroom, which was still arranged and furnished exactly as it had been more than a decade earlier. Well, it wasn't long before *Stacey* began talking about seeing someone in the room...the same as I had years before. At that point, my mother actually placed an open Bible in the little room to 'ward off' whatever was in there."

◆   ◆   ◆

Laura explained that hers wasn't the only "abnormal" house in the neighborhood.

"There were different stories throughout the neighborhood of all kinds of things," she revealed. "One story was about a house that was on the street behind ours, in which a man was supposedly shot to death, way-back-when. We were friends with the children that lived there. The story goes that sometimes, when the owner of the house would come home at night, she would try to put her key in the lock only to find that she couldn't. She could actually feel something resisting her—the key wouldn't even touch the lock. It was as though an invisible hand were blocking the key, trying to keep her from entering the house. There were all kinds of stories of strange goings-on in *that* house, too."

◆   ◆   ◆

Laura's mother still lives in the same house in Lynn, Massachusetts. She has reported no further strange happenings since Laura and her siblings moved out.

"There was never really anything concrete or blatant that happened," she concluded, "but we all have stories of this person we saw in that little back room...and my mother would sometimes see shadows of a person walking through the house when she was alone at night. There was *definitely* something strange about that house...particularly that little back bedroom."

> *Almost as an afterthought, Laura mentioned that, two weeks before she was born, her biological father passed away. Years later, she was told by her mother that the detailed description she used to give of the man in her room matched that of her deceased father...*

The Legend of
Screaming Bridge

It seems that every town has at least one local story that is told and retold around campfires, on stormy nights or at Halloween parties, usually in hushed tones and to wide-eyed listeners. As the following tale illustrates, Arlington, Texas is no exception...

Barbara Holland could easily be described as the "den mother" of our department. She brightens the holidays with homemade treats, fusses if the microwave is left in a mess, and is always ready with a word of advice...or an interesting story.

"It was either the fall of '60 or the spring of '61," Barbara recalled. "I was a freshman at Arlington High School, and my future husband, Brian, was a senior. Some of the boys he hung out with were kind of rowdy, as teenage boys usually are. They would go out on weekends and drink as much beer as possible, and just be generally mischievous. Brian wasn't really a big drinker, so he was usually the designated driver.

"There was this old wooden bridge along a back road on the outskirts of town. One night, when Brian wasn't with them, this group of boys went out drinking, got really intoxicated, and wound up burning down the bridge. As soon as this was discovered, the city had a temporary barricade put up to keep people from driving off into the ravine.

"A few months later, a carload of teenage girls—six of them—were out driving around one Friday night, 'cruising'. Arlington only had one drive-in theater back then; usually, the teens would cruise through there first to see who was out, what was happening, etc., then continue driving around, going nowhere in particular. Well, these six girls eventually wound up on the back road where the burned-out bridge was.

"For some reason, on that particular night, someone had removed the barricade from in front of the bridge. As the girls approached the bridge, they saw some men in the road running toward them and yelling, trying to warn them that the bridge was out. Well, the girls didn't recognize the men and they were unaware that the bridge had been burned out, so they got scared and sped up. Of course, they drove right off the bridge and into the ravine below. Three of the six girls were killed.

"I was at a party at the time. We were playing records, dancing, and just having a good time when we heard the sound of sirens going by. All of a sudden, one of the guys at the party jumped up and said, *'I have to call home!'* He left the party shortly afterwards and we later learned that *his sister had been one of the girls killed in the accident.* Somehow, when he heard the sirens, he sensed that his sister was involved.

"The three girls who survived were never quite the same afterwards. They were a little quieter, and a little more withdrawn. They never talked about the accident."

◆   ◆   ◆

I found out later that, eventually, a permanent concrete structure was built at the site of the old bridge, allowing motorists to safely cross the ravine in which the three girls perished. In the years following the accident, however, there have been reports of strange happenings from people driving in that area. Some have experienced "eerie feelings" while driving along the road at night. Others have reported hearing ghostly screams as they crossed the bridge, which eventually led to the structure being dubbed "Screaming Bridge". Some people still refuse to go anywhere near it.

"I never personally experienced anything unusual," Barbara concluded, "but I *have* heard the stories."

These days, it seems there aren't many people left who know about Screaming Bridge. But something tells me there is still the occasional traveler who wanders through the rural outer perimeter of Arlington in the dead of night and hears the ghostly echoes of a long-forgotten tragedy…

The House on Windy Hill

Our country is rich in history—especially the New England area, site of the original thirteen colonies. We learn of historic figures, structures and events through schoolbooks, documentaries and the like, but sometimes the remnants of history themselves seem to reach out from the past to make their presence known...

A former coworker of mine named John Dennis mentioned to me a while back that he had a couple of stories I might be interested in. Before I could get around to interviewing him, however, he landed a job as a producer in Los Angeles and relocated. With a bit of effort, I was able to connect with him recently for a telephone interview.

"When I was in high school, we lived on a 16-acre farm in Cazenovia, New York," John began. "The farm was off of an old, rural highway and the house itself was a 150-year-old farmhouse, situated on a road called Windy Hill Lane. Originally—many, many years ago—the house was part of the anti-slavery movement known as the 'Underground Railroad'. In the basement, it had secret, underground tunnels that led to the basements of other houses in that area, linking them together. Of course, most or all of these tunnels were sealed off a long time ago for safety reasons. The house we lived in had also been used in the past as a boarding house, or bed and breakfast, where travelers would stay while they were passing through town.

"One stormy afternoon, my two sisters and I had just come home from school. We had taken the bus home, and the house was empty when we got there. Before long, we started hearing strange noises coming from somewhere upstairs—sounds of someone moving around, and what we thought were voices. Of course, we were all freaked out, so I grabbed the nearest weapon I could find—a fireplace poker—and made my way up the stairs with my sisters in tow.

"The noises continued as we walked up the stairs. When we reached the second floor, we peeked around the corner and down the hallway in the direction the noises seemed to be coming from. We saw this weird, misty form, sort of hovering there at the end of the hallway. Well, this *completely* freaked us out and we ran back down the stairs. At that point, we didn't know *what* to think, so we called the police.

"We kept our eyes on the stairs while we waited for the police to arrive. When they finally got there, they made a thorough search of the house, but found nothing. There were no signs of forced entry or anything to indicate that anyone had been in the house, except us. Needless to say, the three of us were completely baffled by the whole thing."

◆   ◆   ◆

Since the house had been a part of the Underground Railroad, I wondered if John had ever experienced anything out of the ordinary in the basement area, where the tunnels were located.

"Yes…there *was* something strange about the basement," he recalled. "I used to have a weight bench down there, so that's where I worked out sometimes. I always had a strange, uneasy feeling when I was down there. It seemed like we were always finding the basement door open, and we'd have to close it and replace the latch, only to find it open again later. There was no way that latch could have worked itself loose or anything, so there was obviously something very strange going on there.

"There were also times when things would disappear and then turn up later in a completely different part of the house. My sisters would ask me about things that were missing, but I had no clue what they were talking about. I might have thought they were just trying to spook me, but it happened to *me* a few times, as well.

"There was a lot of strange activity in that house, but I can't remember all of it...that was a long time ago. What I *can* tell you is that there was definitely something not right about the place...and we never found an explanation for any of the weird things that happened there."

Are the ghosts of the Underground Railroad's "passengers" still hiding out in the house on Windy Hill Lane? Or were the spirits of former boarders responsible for the strange happenings? Whatever the case may be, one thing is certain: The occurrences described in this story were only the beginning of John's experiences with the unknown, as we'll discover in the next...

Carrie's Place

Some spirits seem bound to the places they loved during their lives. These locations seem to offer peace, comfort or sanctuary to the lonely souls, especially when their lives were ended tragically and prematurely...

During my interview with John Dennis, he shared with me a second story—even stranger than the first—involving a sad and untimely death...and the bizarre results.

"I went to college in Bethany, Oklahoma," John explained. "One night, several of my college buddies and I were sitting around, talking. Somehow, we got on the topic of ghosts. Many of the guys had grown up in the Oklahoma City area, and they told me about a nearby haunted school playground, known locally as 'Carrie's Place'.

"The story behind the haunting is that, years ago, there was a woman working at the school—probably a teacher—whose daughter attended the school. Her daughter's name was Carrie. The woman's job required that she stay after school had let out each day to grade papers, or what have you. As she was busy doing this, her daughter would while away the hours on the playground, usually on the swing set. There was one swing in particular that was Carrie's favorite, so she always played on that one swing.

"One evening, after Carrie's mother finished up for the day, she came outside to collect her daughter as usual, but found that she was gone. Sadly, it turned out that she had been abducted and killed. Ever since then, anyone brave enough to go out to that playground at night will sometimes see one of the swings—Carrie's favorite—*swinging by itself.*

"After they told me this story, my buddies decided they would take me to the playground so I could see it for myself. So we went...and I saw it—*one swing in particular was swinging slowly and steadily back and forth.* There was no logical reason for that swing to be moving; the air was still, and none of the other swings were moving—only Carrie's. It was the freakiest thing I had ever seen.

"On several occasions since then, I've taken people out there with me. One time in particular—I think it was Halloween night, actually—several of us climbed into our cars and headed out to Carrie's Place. As we pulled into the playground parking lot, we looked in the direction of the swing set, and we could make out a small figure in Carrie's swing.

"At first, we just thought that there was actually somebody out there playing, which seemed kind of odd to us—that a little kid would be out there alone on Halloween night. But, as we got closer, the figure faded away...leaving only the swing moving back and forth. We just kind of stared at each other in disbelief, then we climbed out of our cars and walked up to the swing. We all stood there and watched it continue to swing...right there in front of us."

I asked John how many times he had been out to Carrie's Place over the years.

"Oh, I must have gone out there fifteen or twenty times," he replied, "and *every single time*, we saw the same thing."

Even a fleeting glimpse into the world of the supernatural can leave us scratching our heads and fumbling for explanations. But after witnessing ghostly activities that occur with the frequency and consistency of a clock's chime...how can there be any doubt that ghosts exist? For John Dennis, at least, there is none...

My Best Friend's Ghost

Most parents never lose their nurturing tendencies, even after their children are grown and have families of their own. Nothing, it seems, can keep these loving parents from looking after their offspring, so long as they live and breathe...and sometimes, even afterwards...

After hearing my former coworker Brian Middleton mention this story just before his transfer to another building, I was intrigued. Several e-mail exchanges later, I was finally able to catch up with him and get the tale in its entirety.

"I grew up in Moline, Illinois," Brian began. "When I was a teenager, my best friend was a girl named Kristy. We used to hang out a lot with our other friends in her basement, which was kind of like a family room. Their house was typical of most houses in that area, with an attic and basement.

"Kristy's father passed away in that house years later, after she had gotten married and moved out. Eventually, she and her husband Steven wound up buying the house and moving back into it.

"Around that time, I was dating a woman who had a little girl named Melissa. The three of us were housesitting for Kristy and Steven one night while they were out. My girlfriend and I spent the evening watching movies while Melissa played downstairs in the basement. Several hours later, Kristy and Steven called and said they were on their way home, so we went ahead and left.

"As far as we knew, that evening had passed uneventfully. I found out a few days later, though, that something very strange had happened. I was talking to Kristy when she asked me, *'Did Melissa enjoy playing with the doll?'* I didn't know what she was talking about, because Melissa hadn't been playing with any dolls that night. I was even more confused when she told me what had happened.

"Apparently, Kristy's mother still had an old doll she'd played with as a child. She kept it buried in an upstairs closet. When Kristy and Steve arrived home that night, they found the doll *on the living room floor*. I told her that we hadn't even been upstairs that night—much less, searching through any closets. We never did find an explanation."

◆   ◆   ◆

"I used to hang out at Kristy's house quite a bit back then. As I said before, the basement was kind of like a family room. It was very spacious, and there was a TV, a pool table and a bar in it. We spent a lot of time down there.

"Sometimes we would hear footsteps overhead, as if someone were wandering around upstairs—even when we were all present and accounted for in the basement. We would go upstairs to check it out, but there was never anyone there. This happened so often that, after a while, we just stopped investigating; we knew we wouldn't find anything if we did."

◆   ◆   ◆

"The strangest thing that ever happened in that house, in my opinion, took place while Kristy and Steven were attending a wedding in Chicago. They had three dogs at the time, and I would usually volunteer to dog-sit while they were away. This time was no exception.

"I would always try to meet them at their house and talk a little bit before they left on their trips, but this time I wasn't able to get there until after they'd left. As a result, I wasn't able to tell them that I'd just had a shift change at work, so I would be staying with the dogs during different hours than they expected.

"As far as I knew, nothing out of the ordinary happened at the house while they were gone. When they got back, though, I found out differently.

"For the first few days of their trip, Kristy would call at least once a day to check on things. Because of my shift change, I was never there when she called. Conversely, I would never hear from her when I *was* there because she thought I was at work, so she didn't call. They always made sure the answering machine was turned off before they went on these trips, so she wasn't able to leave a message.

"Well, after a few days of not being able to reach me, Kristy started to get a little worried, thinking there might be something wrong. Then one day, she called and the answering machine picked up. She was relieved, because she knew I must have been there to turn it on. She assumed everything was okay and didn't call again. The strange thing is that *I didn't turn the answering machine on.* Even stranger is the fact that, when they got home, they found that the machine was once again turned *off,* and there were no messages…not even the one Kristy had left."

Was the spirit of Kristy's father responsible for the strange happenings at her house? Did he retrieve the old doll so that little Melissa might play with it if she came back? Were his the footsteps heard roaming the floor above the basement? Did he turn on the answering machine to ease his daughter's worry? Perhaps these are questions to which we'll never find the answers; the only witnesses were, after all, the doll and the dogs…and none of them are talking…

The Phantom of
Breazeale House

*The term "haunted house" usually conjures up images of a sprawling,
multi-story mansion—one that has stood for at least a century. Though
most of the stories in this book feature no such setting, the following tale
actually does—a 100-year-old, three-story Victorian mansion, in
fact...*

Natchitoches, Louisiana lies in a region of the South known as
"Plantation Country". Within walking distance of this charming little
town's historic district stands a beautiful Victorian mansion called
"Breazeale House" (pronounced like "Brazil"). My wife's friend first
told me about the house, as she is acquainted with the owners; she was
kind enough to put me in touch with them so that I might learn more
about it.

Built for Congressman Phanor Breazeale in the late 1800s, the
house features eleven fireplaces, soaring twelve-foot-high ceilings, nine
stained glass windows, eight bedrooms and three floors, which comprise over 6,000 square feet of living space. According to current owners Jack and Willa Freeman, who opened the house as a bed and
breakfast in 1987, Breazeale House has another, less obvious feature:
The ghost of its original owner.

◆   ◆   ◆

"We lived in the house for some time before we opened it as a bed
and breakfast," Willa explained. "I was the first one to notice that we
weren't alone in the house. Late at night, around 3:00 a.m., I would be

75

awakened by the smell of potpourri—the sweet scent of gardenias. It brought back memories of my grandmother's lawn and the two huge gardenia bushes she had.

"I would get up and try to find out where the smell was coming from. At first, I thought it might be my daughter, Tanya, spraying something in her room, but that wasn't it. Night after night, I would wake up and go in search of the smell. Jack would just roll over and go back to sleep, saying it was my imagination. Eventually, I got tired of the routine, so I gave up.

"Then, someone or something started knocking on the front door. This also happened around 3:00 or 4:00 a.m., and for several nights in a row. I would get up and go downstairs only to find no one at the door. After a few nights of this, Jack started hearing it too, and he'd come downstairs with me. But there was never anyone there. I wasn't getting much sleep at that time; after being awakened around 3:00 a.m., I usually wouldn't bother going back to bed, since I had to get up for school at five o'clock.

"Every day at school, the teachers sitting at my table during lunch would ask me what my ghost had been doing lately. They really thought it was funny. One of the teachers was a preacher's wife. She told me she had read somewhere that if you talk to a ghost and tell it to leave you alone, it will. She also told me to try giving the ghost a name.

"At first, I thought she might just be making fun of me, but what did I have to lose? So, the following night, I put this new theory to the test. As you can imagine, I felt like a fool the first time I did it, but I said, *'Phanor, stop that knocking! Just come on in...you don't need me to open the door.'* To my surprise, it worked—the knocking stopped. And what a relief it was—I could finally get a good night's sleep."

◆　　　◆　　　◆

"For a long time, I was afraid to be alone in the house. When I would come home from school and start doing housework, I often felt like someone or something was following me through the house. One day, I was making a bed upstairs, and I heard my son Tim's door open—the bottom of the door drags across the carpet. I thought he and Tanya were home from school, so I called out to them. When they didn't answer, I looked to see if either of their cars was outside. I saw that neither of them was, and I ran downstairs. I didn't go back up until Jack came home."

◆   ◆   ◆

"We had been in the house almost a year when it came time for the annual Christmas Festival. When we lived in our previous home, we always invited several of our friends over on the day of the festival. We wanted to continue the tradition, so we invited about sixty friends to our *new* home. The house still needed a lot of work at that time, but I couldn't worry about that because we had a festival to enjoy. So, Tanya and I spent a lot of time decorating the house and getting it ready for our guests. We were able to cover up most of the areas that still needed repairs.

"Well, the day of the festival arrived at last. I had electric candles in all my front windows, on all three floors. We had a black cat at that time, and we decided to put it in one of the third floor bedrooms to keep it from getting out during the festival. The carpet was new, so I put down newspapers for the cat. My sister Sarah suggested we unplug the candle in that room because she was afraid the cat might knock it onto the newspaper and start a fire. I told her to remind me when we came back from watching the fireworks display.

"Well, with sixty guests in the house, there's always somebody wanting coffee, or the bathroom, or *something*, so there really wasn't any time for me to worry about the cat. Naturally, I soon forgot about it. A little while later, we were talking and just having a good time in the kitchen, when we heard the sound of a cat meowing in the hot water heater closet. My former daughter-in-law heard it first, and she asked me if I had put the cat in the closet. I told her that the cat was upstairs in one of the third-floor bedrooms.

"Then, we heard the sound again, still coming from the closet. This time, the room was quieter, so everyone heard it. I said that our grandson, Thomas, must have let the cat out. I walked over to the closet and opened the door, but the only thing in there was the hot water heater.

"Jack thought that the cat had somehow gotten out of the room and walked across the attic, then had fallen through the wall. He said, 'Good riddance...I'm not going to tear out a wall to get a silly cat out.' Immediately, I said, 'No, that must be Phanor...he's trying to warn me about the cat knocking the candle over.'

"As I ran up the stairs, I could hear everyone laughing as Jack explained to them how crazy I had gotten since moving into the house. When I got to the third floor and opened the bedroom door, the cat came running out. I looked across the room and saw that *the candle had been knocked onto the newspaper*. I picked it up and knelt down to feel the newspaper—it was already quite hot.

"A cold chill ran up my spine when I thought of what might have happened if we hadn't heard the ghostly cat's meow. As I was walking back downstairs, I stopped for a second, looked up toward the third floor and said, 'Thank you, Phanor.' Ever since that night, I haven't been afraid to stay in the house alone."

◆   ◆   ◆

"Many strange things have happened over the past several years that we can't explain. Probably the strangest of them all happened the week that Dr. Weber died. He was our neighbor.

"Dr. Weber was in his eighties, and he kept to himself most of the time. We had become friends with him, and I loved to visit him and look at his antiques and collectibles. He was a writer, an artist and a collector, and he had taught English at NSU for many years.

"His two children lived out of town, so when they came to make the plans for his funeral, I had arranged for the neighbors to bring some food over to them—this is a southern family tradition. Well, as I was watching the children pack up Dr. Weber's belongings, I thought of how nice it would be to have something to remember him by. It took me a while, but I finally got up the courage to ask them if they would be selling any of his things. They told me that an antiques dealer had taken everything they didn't want off their hands for $300.

"For a minute, I thought I was going to come unglued; even one small item was worth well over that price. But I just calmed down and asked them if I could have a little something of Dr. Weber's as a keepsake. His son told me to look in the closet, because he'd noticed some old dishes with roach powder in them that the antiques dealer had overlooked. I found several glass dishes, two old rocking chairs, and a fountain in the backyard. I paid him and took my findings home.

"The next few nights at Breazeale House were exciting, to say the least. On the first night, Tanya had gone to bed around midnight. She was not yet asleep when she saw a figure come into her room and stand by her bed. At about the same time, I had heard someone walking across her floor. Of course, I thought it was Tanya, getting up to go to the bathroom or something. Well, she was so scared she couldn't scream, so she slid under her covers and stayed there all night.

"Around daybreak, she ran downstairs to tell us what had happened. She made Jack promise to sleep in Tim's room that night—it was right next to Tanya's. This left me downstairs all by myself.

"At one point during the following night, I heard the sound of rainfall. My heart sank, because we had a field trip planned for school the next day. I got up, looked out the window, and saw that it actually *wasn't* raining, although I could *hear* and *smell* rain. I turned on the light and saw water coming down *out of the ceiling*. It was splashing all over the couch and the carpet.

"I was sure a water pipe had burst, so I ran upstairs to get Jack. We hurried up to the third floor together and crawled around on our hands and knees, feeling all the pipes and trying to locate the problem. We never found any leaks…or any explanation for the downpour in my bedroom.

"The next night passed uneventfully…or so we thought. When I came in from school the following day, I got a call from my neighbor. He wanted to know if we'd had guests the night before. I told him we hadn't. He insisted we *must* have, because he'd heard a woman screaming for someone to call the police and that there was a man in her room.

"He said that he and his wife had been awakened by the scream and had called the police. They came out and took a look around, but they didn't find anything out of the ordinary. It was peaceful and quiet, so they assumed that everything was okay. I asked my neighbor to wake us if anything like that ever happened again. After that, things seemed to kind of level off and Tanya finally let Jack move back downstairs, but we never found an explanation for any of this."

◆　　　◆　　　◆

"Several of our guests have also experienced some unexplainable things. Once, we had two sweet old ladies staying on the second floor in the small bedroom. They enjoyed the house very much because it reminded them of the one they grew up in. After they left, I went up to clean their room. As I was dusting the table by the bed, I reached for the potpourri vase and found that it wasn't there. I had just filled it the night before with fresh mulberry potpourri.

"My first assumption was that the scent had been too strong for the ladies, and they had moved the vase to the bathroom. I checked, but it wasn't there. I looked everywhere for it. Tanya had given the vase to me as a Christmas present and she was very upset that it had disappeared. She thought maybe the two ladies had taken it, but I told her not to even think such a thing about those sweet ladies. I thought maybe they had accidentally broken it, and were just too embarrassed to tell us. I was sure they would be sending us a new one within the next few days.

"For several days, Tanya, Jack and I continued to look for the vase, but we had no luck. Then, about a week later, I was standing in the doorway of the room where the ladies had stayed, trying to think of a place we hadn't looked yet. I happened to glance at the table by the bed, and *there was the vase*, bigger than Dallas, as if it had never left.

"I thought Tanya might have been playing a trick on me, so I called her to the door and said, 'I see you found the vase.' She said, 'No...did *you?*' I pointed to the vase and, when she saw it, she screamed. The hair on her arms stood up, and tears were streaming down her face. I said, 'Well, I guess it *wasn't* you.' We never found out where the vase had been or how it got back on the table."

◆   ◆   ◆

"These days, when I'm alone in the house and I hear footsteps, or other strange things happen, I just assume that it's Phanor and I don't worry about it. My family doesn't tease me anymore, because most of them have had an experience or two with Phanor. We can't explain what's been going on in the house since we bought it eight years ago, but I *can* say that it's been exciting and fun. I'm not scared any-more...and I feel that whoever or whatever is in the house only wants what's best for it."

> *Does the ghost of Phanor Breazeale still reside in the bed and breakfast that was once his home? Willa Freeman certainly thinks so...as do, I'm sure, many of the guests who have spent a night or two at Breazeale House.*
>
> *But what about the bizarre, indoor rainfall? And the mysterious screams heard by the neighbors? Could the spirit of the late Dr. Weber have been responsible? If you ever find yourself in the Plantation Country area of Louisiana, perhaps you should spend some time with the Freemans...and try to find out for yourself...*

A Brand-New Haunted House

Many of the stories in this book take place in older structures or loca-tions; as I've stated before, little imagination is required to picture ghosts in these places. But how do you explain a haunting that occurs in a new house—a house with no previous owner, built specifically for you? The following tale involves just such a situation...

The company I work for, like many others, hires contractors to help out when workloads are particularly heavy. One of our more recent contractors, Robert McCray, came in one morning not long ago and began telling my cubicle neighbor a strange tale of the previous evening's events at his home. Of course, having overheard this, I had to catch him on a lunch break and get the whole story.

"I bought a home in Grand Prairie (Texas) about twenty years ago and lived there until recently, when I moved into my current home," Robert revealed. "Many odd things happened in that house; electrical appliances would 'explode' for no good reason; numerous light bulbs would burn out at the same time; I would see figures standing in the hallway, calling out; just very strange things like that.

"I remember one morning, around two o'clock, I was lying in bed, trying to sleep through a thunderstorm. At some point during the storm, I noticed these odd little flashes of lightning 'crawling' through the window and into the room. They formed a little sphere—like ball lightning or something. Very bizarre.

"I would also experience a strange kind of paralysis sometimes while lying in bed. I would just be lying there on my back with my hands folded across my chest, and I would simply be *unable to move*. I remember realizing that I was paralyzed, and desperately trying to move. I would eventually regain my motor skills...slowly."

Things got even weirder, Robert explained, when his *pets* were thrown into the mix.

"One night," he recalled, "I was upset to find that one of my cats, to all appearances, had died. I grabbed a shovel from the garage and, with the other hand, picked up the cat, which was cold to the touch and limp as a dishrag. I was about to put the cat down on a chair when it suddenly came alive in my hand, twisting its body to put its feet down first. As I let go of it, I was stunned. It just turned and looked at me as if it had never been...dead...or whatever it was."

◆   ◆   ◆

Robert went on to say that, after twenty years at his Grand Prairie residence, he was ready to relocate for a change of scenery, a nicer house and a respite from the bizarre activity that had plagued him for years. He soon realized, however, that he would only achieve two of these three goals.

"I've been at my current residence in Plano for about two years now," Robert continued. "The house is brand-new—there were no previous occupants. One of the reasons I was looking forward to moving into a new house was that I'd be getting away from all the strangeness of my old one. Well...it's a *different* strangeness now, but nonetheless, I don't think I managed to escape."

I asked Robert if there had been a previous structure at the site of his new home.

"As far as I know, this was just field land," he replied, "and I haven't heard anything from any of my neighbors about any unusual happenings."

Robert went on to tell me that it wasn't long after his arrival in Plano before he began experiencing a déjà vu of the strangest kind.

"During the move-in," he admitted, "many, many bizarre things went on; most of them I attributed to the house being new. As in my previous house, many of the electrical things seemed to take on a life of their own—the garage door in particular. It would open and close by itself at very odd times. I had an alarm system installed, and *it* began misbehaving. I made several calls to the security service, but they couldn't find anything wrong with the system.

"Many times, the system would indicate that doors or windows were being opened, when they actually weren't. This happened at all hours of the day and night. On several occasions, I was awakened by the sound of the door alarm going off. I would get up out of bed and thoroughly check the house, but I couldn't find the cause.

"The vent fan over the stove would sometimes come on by itself. The intercom system—which is wired to a CD player so that it can pipe music throughout the house—came on by itself one night. My roommate shouted at it and it turned itself off. I sometimes come across very foul odors in some parts of the house; sometimes it's overpowering. There are also areas that are very chilly. Doors open by themselves. There are just all kinds of very odd things going on."

◆   ◆   ◆

Robert went on to say that, over the past several months, much of the strange activity in his house has begun to die down. Although the occurrences have been fewer and farther between, he says, they have been much more unusual.

"One night," Robert recalled, "I was just lying in bed, trying to go to sleep. I had only been there a minute or two when I heard very soft footsteps moving across the carpeting in the bedroom. It was plainly audible; it sounded exactly as though some barefoot person were walking at a normal pace across the pile of the carpet, shuffling slightly.

"My eyes had pretty much adjusted to the darkness and I looked around the room, but I didn't see anyone. Even so, I could still hear the footsteps continuing around the bed...*and coming up the side where I was laying.* It was one of those 'chills-down-the-spine' moments. When the footsteps reached the nightstand, it jostled...*as if it had been bumped.* All the knickknacks on the table rattled as if they had been slightly jarred. At that point, I sat up immediately. I listened for what seemed like several minutes, but the house was quiet after that."

◆   ◆   ◆

I asked Robert if anyone had ever actually *seen* a presence in the house.

"Yes, there *has* been a sighting," he replied. "It was of an older man. He appeared to be over six feet tall, and he was dressed as if traveling—with a heavy overcoat and a fedora. He was seen in the kitchen, standing by the pantry. He turned toward the wall and just vanished right through it. This happened around two o'clock in the afternoon."

I concluded the interview by asking Robert if he had any idea what the source of the activity might be.

"I have no clue," he admitted. "If I knew who or what was responsible, I'd charge them rent."

> *What strange force is behind the bizarre happenings in Robert's past and present homes? Did the "Grand Prairie ghost" follow him to Plano? Was the mysterious figure in the overcoat responsible for all the activity? Or are there others? And perhaps the foremost question in Robert's mind: Will all this "strangeness" follow him to his* next *house?*

Kindred Spirits

The bond between family members, whether they're blood relatives or just very close friends, can be a powerful thing. Some families are so tightly knit that it seems nothing can keep their members from looking after one another...even after death...

Diane Bryan, a friend of mine who works at a major north Texas airport, was taking a cigarette break with a group of her employees one evening when the topic of their conversation turned to ghosts. One of the women in the group named Jocelyn Reynolds revealed that she'd had some very strange experiences in her lifetime. Well, it didn't take long for Diane to put me in touch with Jocelyn so that I could find out more.

"These things have been going on my entire life," Jocelyn confided. "The first thing that comes to mind happened when I was around nineteen years old. I had just moved out of my parents' house. My boyfriend at the time was in the Army, and we had agreed to meet in Amarillo. So I drove myself there and made it okay, but *he* wound up taking a wrong turn somewhere along the way, so I was left there alone for a while. I really didn't have anywhere to go, so I just pulled over and locked myself in the car. I fell asleep waiting for him.

"Around two o'clock in the morning, I woke up to the sound of someone knocking on the car window. It was my boyfriend. As I sat up, I noticed that the interior of my car was filled with the smell of roses. It was very, very strong—unmistakable."

Jocelyn told me that she was bewildered by the incident at the time, but it would later become clear to her what had caused it.

"For the next few years," she continued, "I changed apartments frequently. I would just get tired of living in the same place, so I would pack up my stuff and move to another apartment complex. Well, each time I moved, I would experience the same thing on my first night in a new place: The whole apartment would be filled with the same over-powering scent of roses that I had smelled in my car in Amarillo. It would smell like the place was literally *filled* with hundreds—or thousands—of fresh roses.

"I noticed that, when the rose smell faded, there would be a different smell—cigarettes and musk perfume. That's how I was able to figure out that it was my grandmother, who passed away when I was eight years old. *Grandma was a smoker…and she always wore musk perfume.* You know how everybody's house has a certain smell? Well, my grandmother's house smelled like cigarettes and musk perfume. That was *her* smell. Anyway, this happened *every time* I moved, and *only* when I moved. I guess the rose smell was my grandmother's way of giving me her blessing—kind of like a 'housewarming'—and the musky cigarette smell was her way of letting me know that it was her.

"Around that time, I was dating the man who is now my husband. He never really believed me when I told him about the roses; he just laughed it off and told me I was crazy. When we reached the point in our relationship where we decided to move in together, something happened that changed his mind. We found this older duplex in Dallas that we fell in love with and, while we were in the process of moving in, he encountered the rose smell *himself*. After that, he wasn't so quick to dismiss my stories of strange happenings.

"When we moved into our current home about ten years ago, we *both* encountered the 'housewarming' smell at the same time. It hasn't happened since then, of course, because we haven't moved. But, after all the incidents with the rose smell, I started paying more attention to this sort of thing. I know there were other occurrences earlier in my life, but I had a tendency to just blow them off back then."

◆   ◆   ◆

Jocelyn went on to tell me that she's not the only one in her family who has had strange things happen in her house. Her parents, she confessed, have experienced many unusual occurrences in *their* home as well.

"My parents used to have a cat named 'Kitty'," Jocelyn explained. "They originally hadn't planned to keep him, so they just called him by that generic name. When they actually *did* wind up keeping him, the name just kind of stuck. I'll always remember something very strange that happened to Kitty in my parents' hallway a few years back.

"I was hanging out at their house one day, just lying on the living room couch and watching TV. Now, the layout of the house is kind of important here, so I'll give you a brief description: The TV is situated just a few feet from the door that leads into the hallway; the hallway runs perpendicular to the door, so that if you're walking through the doorway, it runs right-to-left, extending about twenty feet or so to the left, toward the master bedroom, but only about three feet to the right, toward the front bedroom. My mother uses the front bedroom as an office and she keeps the door closed so the cats can't get in there.

"Anyway, I was just lying there watching TV, when I noticed that Kitty was in the hallway, having a fit—hissing and carrying on about…*something*. I remember seeing him walk past the doorway, from left to right, toward the closed office door. The next thing I knew, he was flying through the air in the opposite direction, several feet off the ground. Now remember, there's only about *three feet* of space between the office door and the hallway door—not nearly enough room for Kitty to have gotten up enough speed or momentum to jump like that. I'm five-foot-six, and he was higher than I am tall, so he had to have been close to six feet off the ground.

"Granted, cats *can* jump pretty high from a standstill, but the thing I remember distinctly about this occasion was the fact that, when Kitty went flying across the doorway, there was no *upward* movement whatsoever; he was moving *straight across*. He also had his hind legs tucked underneath him. If he had propelled himself, his legs would have been extended out behind him, obviously.

"After he landed somewhere several feet down the hall, he immediately came running out into the living room, past me, and out the back door into the garage. I still wonder what exactly happened in that three-foot space in the hallway."

I speculated with Jocelyn that there must have been something in the darkened hallway with Kitty, causing him to behave strangely. Given her account, it would appear that some unseen force had actually *picked up* the cat and had *thrown* him down the hall in the opposite direction.

"My mother told me that Kitty had acted that way in the hallway before," Jocelyn admitted, "so there was *definitely* something about it that he didn't like."

◆   ◆   ◆

"As I said before, a lot of strange things have happened at my parents' house over the years. Unfortunately, I can't share them *all* with you because my parents don't feel comfortable with it. We usually only discuss these things amongst ourselves. My sister chooses not to acknowledge it; she definitely knows there's something strange going on—she just chooses to ignore it. My father is very close-mouthed about it, too. He's never told me about anything that's happened to him, but he tells my mother, and *she* tells me. In fact, while we were talking last night, she was telling me that my father has actually *seen* a ghost in their house—I've seen a lot of crazy things in that house, but I've never actually seen a ghost.

"Mom said that it happened the day after Christmas, about three years ago. Dad was sitting on the couch in the living room, reading a book and drinking his tea. It was nice and quiet in the house. At some point he noticed, with his peripheral vision, that someone was sitting in the chair across the room from him. Dad sat perfectly still, moving only his eyes, and he saw the figure of a woman sitting in the chair.

"He couldn't tell who it was at the time, but we've speculated since then that it may have been my grandmother, who died *two* days after Christmas, back in 1974. I think it's also possible that it could have been my best friend Paula; she died very suddenly from a brain aneurysm a few years ago. Paula was very close to my family—my grandmother included. My father has no idea who the figure in the chair was, except that it was a woman."

◆   ◆   ◆

Jocelyn went on to reveal that she frequently has run-ins with mischievous entities in her *own* home...even today.

"I have four sets of keys," she continued. "I've had my keys disappear on me so many times that I had to have duplicate sets made. There's nothing more frustrating than trying to leave for work and not being able to find your keys. Other small household items have disappeared, as well.

"What's weird is that these things always turn up sooner or later...usually within a few days, and *always* in very odd places. I've found them in pasta bowls, cookie jars, tennis shoes, and bathroom drawers—even on the top shelf of the kitchen pantry, which *never* gets used. I don't waste my time or energy looking for them anymore...I know they'll show up sooner or later."

I asked Jocelyn if she had any theories regarding the identity of the prank-pulling spirit or spirits.

"I kind of think it's Paula, picking on me," she reflected. "I suppose it might also be my brother-in-law, who passed away suddenly last year. Or maybe even my grandmother. Sometimes I think the three of them just sit up there and think, 'Okay, how are we going to mess with Jocelyn today?'"

Stories such as this make it difficult to deny the existence of ghosts. But, whether you're a believer or a skeptic, perhaps the next time you pass by a garden, you'll remember to stop and smell the roses...

A Gettysburg Ghost

So little is known about the shadowy realm in which ghosts exist; for all we know, the laws of time and distance that govern our world may not apply in the afterworld. Clearly, there are countless examples of phantom encounters in which logic, as we know it, seems to be conspicuously absent. For many of those who witness such encounters, this lack of reason makes an already unsettling experience all the more terrifying, as we'll examine in this next story...

During my interview with Jocelyn Reynolds, she shared with me an intriguing tale of an apparent *long-distance* haunting.

"My parents have lived in the same house in Euless for 36 years—ever since I was born," Jocelyn began. "My dad is retired, so he and my mom do a lot of traveling these days. Since my husband and I also live in Euless, we usually keep an eye on their house while they're away.

"One of my parents' favorite destinations is the historic area in and around Gettysburg, Pennsylvania. They've gone there every year for about the past six years. Now, as I said before, there has *always* been a lot of strange activity in my parents' house. I don't know if it's because my grandmother passed away there or what, but it's never been anything bad; I mean, there were never any 'negative vibes' there. But, for some strange reason, whenever Mom and Dad are visiting the Gettysburg area, a *different* presence seems to get stirred up. It's one we're not familiar with, and it seems kind of ominous—almost threatening.

"Anyway, while my parents were on last year's 'annual pilgrimage', I went to check on their house as usual, around 4:30 in the afternoon. I walked around to the rear of the house so I could go in through the back door. Now, I *know* how to get in and out of my parents' house;

I've done it my entire life. But for some reason that night, I *could not* get in. Their back door has two locks—the doorknob lock and a dead-bolt. I unlocked them both, but the door still wouldn't open. I thought maybe I had turned one of the locks the wrong way, actually locking what was unlocked to begin with, so I double-checked them both. I still couldn't get in.

"I spent about *fifteen minutes* trying to get in that door, which I can normally do in my sleep. The weird thing was that, even when I *knew* both locks were unlocked, I couldn't even turn the doorknob; *it felt like someone was holding it in place*. I could also feel resistance against the door itself, as if someone on the other side was applying outward pressure to it.

"Nothing *this* crazy had ever happened at that house, so my natural assumption was that someone had broken in…which, of course, scared me half-to-death. So I went to the neighbor's house and had them call the police. When they arrived, the door opened right up—no problems whatsoever. They searched the house and found nothing out of place, nothing missing, no signs of forced entry, no broken locks…nothing. I was really embarrassed, but the police officers were really nice about it. Then, as they were leaving, one of them asked me *if the house was haunted*. That really caught me off guard. I'm still not really sure why, but I lied and said that it wasn't.

"I found out later that, at the same time I was trying to get in the back door, my father was on the Antietam Battlefield, walking up and down Bloody Lane."

The Battle of Antietam took place in September of 1862, outside the small, historic town of Sharpsburg, Maryland. It marked the first of two attempts by Confederate General Robert E. Lee to take the Civil War onto northern soil. The battle became known as the single blood-iest day of the entire war, with combined casualties of 23,100 wounded, missing and dead.

With such a tragic history, it's no wonder the Antietam Battlefield is reported to be thick with the ghosts of soldiers who died there. The area known as "Sunken Road" or "Bloody Lane" is said to be the *most* haunted place on the battlefield. This country road, which once divided the property of two local farmers, eventually became the center of the battle; it served as a rifle pit for two Confederate brigades. The order was given that the road be held at all costs. The Federals tried repeatedly to take the road, but unit after unit fell back under the barrage of fire from the Confederate position.

Eventually, the Union troops gained a vantage point from which they could fire down upon the road's defenders. For the Federals, this was like shooting animals in a slaughter pen; before long, the road was filled with bodies, stacked four and five deep. Over the years, Bloody Lane has become known as one of the eeriest places on the battlefield. Witnesses have described sounds of phantom gunfire, ghostly shouting, and the inexplicable smell of gunpowder.

"It seems like every time my parents visit that area," Jocelyn explained, "there is strange activity in their house. I don't really understand the connection—why my parents being in or near Gettysburg causes unrest in their house hundreds of miles away—but it's gotten to the point where *nobody* wants to go over there while they're gone.

"The last time they were in Gettysburg, a few weeks ago, I went over to their house around 3:30 in the afternoon to feed the cats. I walked into the garage and flipped the light on. When I was about halfway across the garage, the light went out. I thought maybe I hadn't flipped the switch all the way up, so I turned around and started back toward it. Before I got there, *the light came back on.* I flipped the switch down and then up again, making sure it was all the way on.

"A few minutes later, while I was feeding the cats, the light went out *again.* I said aloud, *'Okay…we're not going to play this game,'* and it came *back on.* I finished what I was doing and got ready to leave. I decided not to worry about checking the rest of the house—I was ready to get out of there.

"I went through the utility room and out the back door, leaving the porch light on. As I walked away from the house, the *porch* light went out. I walked back to the door to unlock it so I could turn the light back on. As soon as my key was in the lock, *the light came back on again.* When I finally got in my car, the hair on the back of my neck was standing up.

"What's really weird is that, when my parents are visiting anywhere else, everything is perfectly normal at their house. They can be in San Antonio and I can go over there at ten o'clock at night and not have any problems whatsoever. Why there is activity when they're in the Gettysburg area, we have no idea. But then, I guess *nobody* really knows the 'hows' and 'whys' of this kind of thing."

> *What is the mysterious connection between the historic Antietam Battlefield's "Bloody Lane" and the unassuming Euless, Texas residence of Jocelyn's parents? My research into the history of the battlefield revealed that a certain group of soldiers from New York known as the "Irish Brigade" played a major role in the onslaught at Bloody Lane. Jocelyn's mother, it turns out, is Irish. Is it possible that one of her ancestors fought and died on that fateful September day so long ago? Is it he who is responsible for the bizarre activities that Jocelyn encountered? Or is the explanation for all of this simply beyond the comprehension of the living? If you plan to visit the Gettysburg area, make it a point to walk along Bloody Lane. Perhaps, upon your return home, you'll discover that you, too, had an unexpected guest while you were away...*

Lost and Found

In previous stories, we've examined how loved ones who've passed on can still sometimes bridge the gap between their world and ours in order to ease the troubled minds of the living. The following tale involves another such case of this kind of transcendence.

When my mother-in-law, Kim Prikryl, found out I was writing this book, she mentioned an incident involving her best friend of 37 years, Patti Tunnell. Patti had recently moved into a new house in the same neighborhood that Kim and her husband had lived in for nearly a decade. With a bit of coaxing (and Kim's cooperation), I was able to get Patti's full account.

"When my father passed away in 1985," Patti explained, "my mother wanted each of her three daughters to have something my dad had given her. She gave me a pair of diamond stud earrings that he had once given her as an anniversary present. I cherished them, and I wore them quite often.

"Several years later, my home was burglarized. The thief emptied out my jewelry case, but one of the earrings had snagged the lining and was left behind. I continued to wear the single earring, because it was still a reminder of my father."

◆　　　◆　　　◆

"A few years ago, my mother's mental health began to fail, and she had to enter a nursing home. Her condition continued to worsen, and we all took turns visiting her. Naturally, we assumed that she was getting quality care. Well, after about a year in the nursing home, Mother developed pneumonia and we had to put her in the hospital.

"While she was there, the nurses told us that she was showing signs of neglect. Evidently, the nursing home staff had not been turning her in bed or caring for her skin properly, so she had developed bedsores. The nurses at the hospital suggested we take legal action against the nursing home, and we did. Shortly after we initiated the lawsuit, Mother passed away. About a year later, we received a large settlement.

"After much soul-searching, my husband Steve and I decided to use some of the money to buy a new home down the street from my best friend, Kim. Well, for the first few weeks after moving into our new home, I was very distraught. I cried a lot, and I often wondered if we had done the right thing.

"Then, one day while I was cleaning my bathroom, I stepped on something sharp. I couldn't see what it was, so I shrugged it off and started to walk away, but something stopped me. For some strange reason, I felt like I should look harder for whatever it was I'd stepped on. I got down on my hands and knees and soon found it—my diamond earring. I carried it to the bedroom to put it away, wondering how it wound up on the bathroom floor.

"When I opened my jewelry case, I was surprised to see the earring already inside. That's when the hair on the back of my neck stood up...*I had just found the mate to my mother's diamond stud earring!* I picked up both earrings and took a deep breath. At that moment, I felt a strange calmness wash over me; I knew that this was a sign from my mom and dad that I *had* 'done the right thing'—the new house was just what they had wanted for me. In the time since then, this house has become the most serene and comforting home I've ever lived in."

Skeptics might argue that the earring Patti found was simply left behind by the previous owners of the house and just happened to match her mother's—but what are the odds? And how could the earring have lain undetected on the bathroom floor for weeks before it was discovered? Why was Patti the one who discovered it? For Mrs. Tunnell, at least, these questions have a very simple—and very comforting—answer.

Haunted Savannah

One might not expect a writer of stories about ghosts to be terribly sur-
prised upon discovering he's recently been in the company of them. But,
expectations aside, I was quite taken aback when I found myself exam-
ining freshly printed evidence that I had indeed come within close
proximity of my subject matter—evidence without which I never
would have known...

My wife and I spent our honeymoon in the beautiful and historic
city of Savannah, Georgia last summer. This charming port city is
probably best known contemporarily as the backdrop for the popular
novel and major motion picture *Midnight in the Garden of Good and*
Evil. Unbeknownst to many, Savannah also boasts the reputation of
being the second most haunted city in the U.S. (Salem, Massachusetts
being the first).

Although my wife might argue otherwise, I was unaware of this dis-
tinction when I chose the city as our honeymoon destination. Of
course, as long as we were there, we couldn't bypass the opportunity to
experience one of the many "ghost tours" offered throughout the city.
The tour we chose consisted of a nocturnal carriage ride through some
of the more infamous parts of town, with our driver acting as guide
and storyteller as we clip-clopped over the ballast stone streets and
through the ambience of Savannah after sundown.

Later that night, upon returning to our bed and breakfast (a 150-
year-old Victorian mansion), we couldn't help wondering if there
might be a spirit or two wandering the hallways *there.* We agreed to
keep an eye out for unusual happenings during the remainder of our
stay, but we noticed nothing unusual—until, that is, we returned
home.

We had taken many photos during our honeymoon and were anxious to see how they turned out, so we had our film developed at a nearby one-hour photo-processing center. A short while later, we were finally settled in at home, relaxing and enjoying the photos. Most of them were fairly ordinary (the considerable beauty of Savannah's architecture, flora and stately squares notwithstanding), but when we came to the photos we'd taken in the lobby of our bed and breakfast, we immediately noticed something strange. One photo in particular—a nice shot of my wife in an evening dress sitting next to a window—showed the vague outline of what appeared to be *a hooded figure* standing outside the window. The figure was ghostly pale, with indistinct features; two dark areas marked the eye sockets and a third seemed to be a gaping mouth. Oddly, even though its features were unclear, my wife and I both felt that the figure's expression seemed somehow *menacing*.

We laughed about it at first, writing it off as the pattern of leaves on the tree outside the window. But, upon closer inspection, I noticed a *second* figure; it was very near the first and *also* appeared to be wearing a dark, hooded robe. This second figure had features that were clearer than those of the first, with a discernible nose, mouth and eye sockets, all of which had the proper proportions required to be a human face. Stranger still, the second figure's *hands* were visible and seemed to be pressed together just below its chin, in an attitude of prayer or meditation. We wondered...*could these have been monks?*

Also visible through the window in the photo was the building across the street from our bed and breakfast, which was a very old structure itself. We had walked past it the previous evening, but couldn't determine whether it had been a residence, a business...or possibly a *church* of some sort.

Whatever the explanation behind the mysterious figures in the photograph may be, one fact remains: My wife and I had a wonderful time in Savannah, and we plan to go back some day. For now, at least, we're content just knowing that we came away with such an intriguing and unusual souvenir.

> *Finding a "figure" in the background of a photograph can sometimes be accomplished with little more than a good imagination. But when two figures can be seen—very near one another and apparently wearing identical clothing—how can we resist entertaining the thought that we may actually have captured one of mankind's greatest mysteries on film?*
>
> *Savannah's timeless mystique will undoubtedly still be intact when my wife and I return there some time in the near future...and yes, we will be taking the camera...*

0-595-29786-2